END OF THE PIER

The fifth novel in my
'Tales from Great Yarmouth'
series

Tony Gareth Smith

http://www.fast-print.net/bookshop

End of the Pier

ISBN: 978-178456-635-7

All characters are fictional.
Any similarity to any actual person is purely coincidental.

A catalogue record for this book is available from the British Library

First published 2019 by
FASTPRINT PUBLISHING
Peterborough, England.

This novel is dedicated to the memory of
Betty Florence Beadle.
Skittles and Golf have never been the same.

Also by Tony Gareth Smith

Twice Nightly - 2012
To Catch a Falling Star - 2014
Curtains - 2015
Backstage - 2017
Short stories – The Landladies Convention and Boarding
Tonight

Website
www.twicenightly.net
E-mail Tony
tonygarethsmith@twicenightly.net

End of the Pier

Chapter One – January

A thick fog hung over the shores of Great Yarmouth, Gorleston and Brokencliff-on-Sea. The damp air made those out walking their dogs think of log fires and hot buttered toast. The shoppers in Great Yarmouth were wrapped in their winter best, sporting gaily coloured scarves and hats, Christmas gifts from maiden aunts that they rarely saw. There were fewer stalls open on the market and with the cold snap due to continue, there was a general consensus that snow was on the way. The smell of freshly cooked chips lured some shoppers to partake of a bag, dowsed in salt and vinegar, as soon as the stalls opened, , their cold hands picking the golden sticks and putting them into their eagerly awaiting mouths.

Along the seafront, work had commenced on the Golden Sands Pier and Theatre and heavy plant of machinery could be seen. Workmen in their thick overalls and hard hats chatted as they worked, all hoping that the cold spell would break and give them some respite from the North Sea lapping hungrily at the base of the pier. Flasks filled with hot soup, coffee and tea were their only comfort until the gaffer called a break in the day's work.

Proprietors of the amusement arcades, cafés and shops surveyed the paint work that would need doing before the advance of the Easter and Summer seasons were upon them. They concentrated their efforts on the interiors in need of deep cleansing. Tables and chairs would be replaced where necessary, arcades would exchange slot machines for newer models and shops would look at their stock, reducing any for a quick sale when the business was reopened. Trips to wholesalers and visits from reps were the order of the day. Even when the money wasn't rolling in, business continued behind the scenes.

The funfairs would see a fresh lick of paint and, if funds were available, a new ride or two. The gardens, once resplendent in beautiful flora and fauna lay barren until the warmer months when they would come alive again with uniformed patterns. The horses and ponies that provided the rides were in their winter quarters, being lovingly cared for by their owners and enjoying a well-earned rest from the toil of standing in summer temperatures for hours on end while waiting their next fare.

Poster hoardings were covered with advertisements for winter sales, coach excursions and local cinema offerings until the stars of stage, screen and circus were advertised in their twice daily/nightly shows. Everything was wrapped in its winter coat until the warmer days of spring blossomed once more.

At Brokencliff-on-Sea, adjacent to Gorleston-on-Sea and between Gorleston and Hopton-on-Sea, Sadie and Roberto Casalino were settling in at The Fisherman's Arms. They had decided that they would advertise for staff to help during the busy evening shifts and also the weekend lunchtime period when business was brisk. Sadie intended to offer filled rolls as well as the usual bar snacks of nuts and crisps. She had ruled out Roberto's idea of providing hot food, even though the pub had a fully equipped kitchen. She had done some ground work and found that the previous tenants had only offered hot food on special occasions and that the menu was very limited. Sadie was conscious of treading on the toes of others who provided food, thinking mainly of The Toasted Teacake which was nearby.

One evening, a lady sat at the bar with a gin-and-tonic and a bag of crisps. Roberto had served her with his usual Italian charm.

"It is a shame you don't have live music in here," said the lady, who was smartly dressed for the inclement winter weather.

"When we had a bar in Brighton, we often had live music," Roberto replied.

"What kind of music do you like?"

"I love Italian love songs and of course some of the pop stuff isn't too bad."

Without any warning the lady began to sing an Italian song that Roberto recognised; Sadie who was out the back came into the bar and watched. The song was *Malafemmena*, a man's song to a woman who drives him crazy and then deceives him.

Roberto was amazed; her pronunciation and pitch were perfect and it brought a tear to his eye.

"Bravo, bravo! Where did you learn to sing like that?"

"I am a professional singer. Allow me to introduce myself, I am Donna Quinn."

Sadie clapped and walked over to Donna. "That was beautiful. Do you know many Italian songs?"

"Plenty, and if I don't I only have to hear a recording a few times and I can learn them quickly."

Donna handed them both a business card. "These are my contact details. I can be booked via Rita's Angels if you are interested."

"We met Rita at the New Year's Eve party, Roberto. You remember, the lady who is getting married."

Roberto smiled. "Ah yes, the beautiful lady in the shimmering gown."

Donna picked up her handbag. "I really must go as I have an appointment, but as I say, if you want to book me, you have the details." She turned to go. "Oh, just one thing, you would need to provide a piano, I don't have my own band."

"No problem," said Roberto. "We are having our piano delivered next week from our last establishment."

Donna said her goodbyes and left the pub.

"Well Roberto, my love," said Sadie, squeezing her husband's buttocks and going back behind the bar. "We mustn't let that one get away, she could help put us firmly on the map."

* * *

Reverend George hurried as best he could along the snowy pavements of Brokencliff-on-Sea and headed for the main road to catch a bus into Lowestoft. His 'daily', who was clearing the pavement of snow outside the rectory, watched him as he went. 'He'll go arse-over-tit, if he's not careful' she thought to herself. 'Always in a rush, one day he will meet himself coming back.' She banged her broom against the fence and looked up.

"More snow in them clouds, or my name's not Martha Tidwell," she said out loud. A robin who had just settled on the fence, chirped as if in agreement. She looked at the little bird and began to make a hole in the snow, revealing the frozen earth below. She went to the garden shed and, using a trowel, began to break the earth as best she could. The robin cocked his head

4

on one side and watched her. When she had finished, Martha stood to one side and her newly acquainted friend hopped down from the fence and began to prod the earth with his beak in the hope of finding a worm or some morsel that he could enjoy.

Martha smiled. "You have a rummage in there, my dear and I will go and see if I have a packet of bird seed in my bag; it's for my Joey, but he won't mind sharing some with the likes of you."

The robin chirped and continued to dig away quite happily.

The Reverend just made it to the bus stop in time and boarded the number one. He smiled at the driver and made his way to the top deck. As the bus pulled away, he looked out at the scene of white, which had covered the countryside hedges and fields. Rooftops were glistening in the weak sunshine that was trying to break through the clouds. He pulled an envelope from his coat pocket and again read the letter, still puzzled by the content. He was requested to attend the offices of Wicker, Coombe and Brown, solicitors in Lowestoft. He read the letter again and putting it back in the envelope returned it to his coat pocket.

"Mr Wicker, the Reverend George is here to see you."

Mr Wicker looked up from his desk and moved a couple of files. "Thank you, Miss Benson, please show the gentleman in and bring in tea for two."

Miss Benson nodded.

"Reverend George, thank you so much for coming in to see me," said Mr Wicker shaking the Reverend by the hand. "Please have a seat."

Reverend George sat down. "I have to say Mr Wicker I was surprised to receive your letter and slightly intrigued too. It isn't often I get invited to see a solicitor."

Mr Wicker smiled. "It is nothing to worry about. To the contrary it is, I believe, to your advantage."

Miss Benson brought in a tea tray and closed the office door.

"Please help yourself to milk and sugar, Reverend George. Now let me give you some information. You will be familiar with a Miss Sayers?"

"Yes of course, oh dear me, nothing has happened to her has it, only when I left my last parish we did keep in touch, but I haven't heard from her for some weeks and due to my own demanding schedule, she was on my 'to do' list."

"Well, I am sorry to be the bearer of sad tidings but Miss Sayers passed away a few weeks ago. She had been suffering with her heart and, of course, she was in her nineties."

The Reverend nodded and paused before answering. "She was a lovely lady and very supportive of the church."

"Miss Sayers' solicitors have been in touch with me, I happen to know a couple of the partners; we went to university together. Miss Sayers thought a lot of you, Reverend George and, to that end, has left you a considerable sum of money, some would say a fortune."

Reverend George was startled by the news. "But surely, her own family…?"

"Her two remaining relatives have been provided for and there were several donations to various charities she favoured. The dear lady had shares in various companies and had the odd flutter, I understand."

"I don't know what to say," said the Reverend, stirring his tea.

Mr Wicker glanced at the file in front of him. "This is the sum that has been left to you." Mr Wicker pushed a piece of paper across the desk.

"Oh, my goodness. Surely this can't all be for me?"

"I can assure you that it is," he replied. "I will need certain particulars from you so that a transfer of funds can be arranged. If you need any advice on investing some of the capital then I would be happy to guide you."

The Reverend was quite taken aback. "Oh, my goodness gracious! I don't know what to say."

"There is also a letter addressed to you from Miss Sayers which you will want to read privately at your own leisure. There is only one stipulation and that is you use the money wisely and enjoy yourself. Miss Sayers was well aware that you haven't always been happy in your profession due to some personal difficulties which you confided with her. Perhaps some more tea, vicar?"

Reverend George nodded, this really couldn't have come at a better time, as he was planning to give up his diocese and had no idea where he would live when he vacated the vicarage.

"As it so happens I was planning on giving up my ministry, I feel my life is leading me in a new direction."

Mr Wicker nodded. "So this offer would seem to have come at the right time."

"Oh yes it has."

"Let's enjoy our tea, Reverend George while you reflect on the news. I am sure you may have many questions."

Taking a large mouthful of tea, Reverend George sat back in the chair feeling somewhat overwhelmed by it all.

* * *

There had been another heavy snowfall, but Reverend George was determined to keep his appointment. His cleaner, Martha's gallant efforts to clear his pathway had been covered again in a white dusting and he gingerly made his way down the road, pulling his scarf tighter to keep out the wind blowing off the North Sea. It reminded him of the terrible winter of '63 when the River Yare had been frozen over, making it seem possible to skate across from Gorleston to Great Yarmouth. With his head bowed, he continued his journey; it wasn't too far now and he could see the lights of the public house gleaming in the distance.

Over a pint in the Fisherman's, Joe Dean, owner of Finnegan's Wake Caravan Park listened as Reverend George told his story. "Charles, that is wonderful news. Congratulations, I am very pleased for you."

"There is a lot to organise, I have to see the Bishop next week and then there will be the question of me handing over the reins to a new vicar."

"Well it certainly is all change," said Joe, supping his pint. "Things are beginning to take shape across the road; most of the vans have been removed and work is about to begin on building the chalets. I think everything should be ready for the forthcoming season, if not Easter."

"Joe, how would you feel about sharing a home with me? I could look for something away from Brokencliff and you could put a caretaker in the park to oversee things."

Joe looked at Charles "It is something I would need to think about carefully Charles, we don't want to start any unnecessary gossip."

"I will say no more, but it would be a nice idea, wouldn't it?"

Joe nodded, he knew they had both been skirting around the mutual attraction they held for each other for a long time, maybe it was right that they should move on with a life together in the proper sense.

* * *

Lucinda Haines had decided it was time for a visit to the hairdressers and was greeted at the salon by Mr Adrian. "Good morning Lucinda, it is so lovely to see you. Maddie get Miss Haines a coffee and a biscuit."

He took Lucinda's coat and showed her to a chair.

"Thought I needed tidying up," said Lucinda, smiling. "Everyone liked what you did for me last time."

"And we can soon have you looking wonderful again," said Mr Adrian showing off his pearly white teeth. "How have you been keeping?"

"One mustn't grumble," said Lucinda. "Just the usual things that come along as we get older."

"The weather has been quite awful, hasn't it?" said Mr Adrian, running his fingers through Lucinda's hair and examining the ends. "I fairly skidded the other morning coming out of the house. I am always afraid of falling over."

"Yes, it is a hazard," said Lucinda, "but we must expect snow at this time of the year. Some countries have it a lot worse than we do."

"Arh, here's our Maddie with your drink. You sit and relax there a while and then Maddie will give you a wash. I'll go and fetch my box of tricks from the office and we'll have you looking like the belle of the ball in no time."

Retreating to his office, Mr Adrian lit a cigarette and took a deep draw. It had been quite a busy morning and he was feeling a little tired. He took some Pro Plus from his desk drawer and swallowed them with some water, knowing that they would at least keep him awake. He had had friends over the night before, things had got a little out of hand, and he was feeling the after-effects of it now. He looked out of the door at Lucinda and thought that she didn't look too well, but he knew better than to pry; Lucinda Haines wasn't one to share much information, although he found her a delightful lady. She would often listen to his troubles and he felt she never judged him unlike some of the previous ladies he had put his faith in. Shirley Llewellyn sprung to mind, but she was long gone from the area. He made a quick phone call to his suppliers, querying a delivery and then, eyes and teeth, he emerged from the office like a butterfly from a chrysalis.

"Now my dear lady, let us get started. Maddie, a wash for Miss Haines please and use some of the new coconut conditioner." He touched Lucinda's shoulder with a gentle squeeze and smiled.

"I am fed up with this weather," said Freda Boggis, walking gingerly along the pavement.

"They say it should begin to thaw at the end of the week," said Muriel Evans taking Freda's arm to steady them both. "Have you much to get at Mrs Jary's?"

"One or two things that I can't get at the cash and carry," said Freda. "Dick likes her ham, so I'll get some of that and I am out of pickle; he likes a bit of pickle, does my Dick."

Mrs Jary greeted the two ladies as an icy blast came through the shop door.

"Good morning, ladies and how are we today?"

"Like two penguins without a woolly hat between us," said Freda.

"Do penguins wear hats?" queried Mrs Jary with a grin.

"They do in those cartoons they keep putting in the paper," said Freda "I wonder how they knit them, must be awkward with those flippers."

Muriel gave a knowing look to Mrs Jary. "I expect the Eskimos do it for them."

"Oh yes, I never thought of that," replied Freda. "Can I have a quarter of your nice ham, Mrs Jary, a quarter of tea and a jar of sweet pickle."

Mrs Jary went to the meat slicer.

"I think I might treat myself to a coconut sponge," said Muriel. "I meant to bake a cake yesterday, but somehow I never got around to it."

"My oven's on the blink again, I've told Dick we need to get a new one. If the weather ain't too bad tomorrow, I'll pop over to the Gas House and see what they have got on offer, bound to be something in their sale."

"Yes, I have to say I do prefer gas to electric," said Muriel. "I couldn't get on with my electric cooker, couldn't get to grips with the temperatures. Gas is far simpler."

"Can I get you anything else?" asked Mrs Jary.

"I think I will take a couple of packs of biscuits," said Freda, selecting a couple from the shelves. "That should do me for now."

"I see you have got pork chops," said Muriel. "I'll have a couple of those please, save me going to the butchers. I need a loaf of bread, half a pound of butter and some of your nice Cheddar cheese, not that Red Leicester stuff; Barry didn't care for that."

"I am surprised," said Mrs Jary. "It's a popular seller."

"Sadly not in our house," said Muriel, "and I best take a bottle of Fairy."

"Mind how you go," said Mrs Jary as the two left the shop laden with their goods. "It is quite slippery out there this morning."

"Fancy," said Freda with a huff. "As if we didn't know that walking here."

Everyone was hoping that the weather would ease up, but following the long-awaited thaw, more snow was on the way and it looked like being a very cold month. Traffic struggled getting into the town, traffic lights failed and some of the country roads were impassable. But, being British, they soldiered on, even if they did complain to their loved ones and friends.

Rita Ricer sat in her office at Rita's Angels and began making a list of who to invite to the wedding, what venue to choose and whether or not it should be a church or registry office.

Malcolm Farrow had been busy at The Sparrow's Nest in Lowestoft and the two were passing ships in the night. Rita had never stayed the night at his home in Oulton Broad, nor he at hers. There was no doubt that Rita was smitten with Malcolm but doubts often crept in when she thought of her late husband Ted. Malcolm and Ted were poles apart in every respect.

Jenny Benjamin interrupted her thoughts by bringing in a copy of *The Stage and Television Today*.

"Sorry to butt in," she said, "but there is a lovely article on Derinda Daniels and Ricky Drew. The dancer recruit ad has gone in. Doreen and Jill are keen to get some new blood on board."

Rita took off her glasses and looked up. "Well, there should be plenty of choice out there with all the shows that will need to be covered across the country. How many are the Dancing School providing for?"

"They have offers on six for certain," said Jenny, "and then, if the Golden Sands is back in business by the summer, they hope to get first refusal on the show there."

"I wouldn't count on that," said Rita. "There is still no word on who will be running the pier once it has been rebuilt. Tell Doreen and Jill to put the feelers out for Skeggy and Morecombe, they may have some luck there."

Chapter Two – February

Philippa Tidy of Tidy Stores at Brokencliff-on-Sea was checking in an order of new stock when the door bell sounded. It was Joe Dean.

"Morning Joe, it's a bit parky out there today."

There was a low bark and the patter of feet as Dingle came out from behind the counter wagging his tail and sat down, paw in the air, looking at Joe.

"Hello old boy, come and see your Uncle Joe. If you are very good and Mummy says that I can, I will take you for a walk later."

"You'd be doing me a favour," said Phil. "At least the snow has gone and it's quite dry out there at the moment. I haven't the energy to go far today, fighting off a cold I think.

Joe rubbed his hands. "It's certainly the weather for it. I've come to collect my grocery order if it's ready."

"Of course, I have it in a box out the back. I'll just go and get it. Is everything okay with you? I see the builders have been doing a sterling job on the park."

"Oh, they've been coming along champion, despite the weather which didn't seem to bother them. I hope to see it all finished by March, might just make the Easter weekend."

Phil put the box on the counter. "You are all settled so there is nothing to pay. Are you okay, you look a bit down?"

"I had some news that has unsettled me a bit. Reverend George is giving up the parish and is thinking of moving away, though that isn't common knowledge."

Phil, who wasn't one to mince words, spoke openly. "So where does that leave you? I know you two are very close."

Joe blushed. He had always thought that Phil knew more than she let on. "It's a tricky situation. I'm just getting the caravan site sorted out; it isn't something I can just abandon."

"The Rev wants you to go with him, is that what you're saying?"

"Well yes and no, you see we have always been very close friends and he is thinking that maybe we should live together."

"Look Joe, tell me to mind my own business, but I have long been of the opinion that you and he are a little bit more than friends."

"Well, we would like to be, that is to say, I would like us to be."

"So, what on earth is stopping you?"

"Well, you know how people gossip and I wouldn't want either of our names dragged through the mud. Charles has been a pillar of the community and his decision to leave the Church is his own affair, I have played no part in that."

"Couldn't he move in with you at Finnegan's?"

"I think that would be too close for comfort, besides I have the business to run, I am not sure what Charles would turn his hand to, he will obviously want to do something. He has suggested buying a property out of Brokencliff, but then that would mean me not being where I am needed."

"I think you need to be with each other by the sounds of things. You could always put a night watchman in place at the park or a telephone line that would come through to you so that you could come back at a moment's notice, should the need arise. When has the Rev to be out of the vicarage?"

"As soon as they have appointed someone I suppose, I don't fully understand the process, but I expect Charles would stay on to induct the new person."

Phil sighed. "He is taking a big step, a leap of faith you might say, but then if you both did it together it would be better for both of you. Times have changed, or are changing, men sharing a home together is no big deal these days and what your preferences are in bed are of no concern of anybody else's."

"That's one hurdle we haven't yet accomplished."

"Well that's for further down the track, at least no one can say you have gone into it just for the sexual thrill."

Joe blushed again. "I don't want to let him down. He has been a great friend to me."

"And you to him, now don't you forget that. What was it that Mother Abbess said in the sound of music? When God closes a door, somewhere he opens a window."

"Thanks for listening Phil, you're a true pal."

"Oh, be getting away with you. Tell you what, why don't you and Charles come over to me this evening for supper and I'll open a bottle of wine."

"Thanks Phil, that would be grand. I will have to check with Charles first. I'll give you a call and let you know. Don't worry Dingle, I'll be back for you later."

Dingle gave a small bark.

Phil opened the door and watched as Joe left the shop, carrying his box of groceries and wished him, in her heart of hearts, all the luck in the world.

"Did you get any Valentine cards?" Muriel asked Freda while they were enjoying a small sherry one evening in Freda's sitting room.

"Not even the sniff of one," said Freda with feeling. "I can't remember the last time my Dick gave me anything for Valentine's Day. Hang on a minute, yes I can, once he gave me a packet of Daz.."

"He gave you packet of washing powder for Valentine's?"

"As sure as I am sitting here, said it was to bring sparkle into our lives. I gave him sparkle alright, I handed him some Windolene and told him to get cleaning the windows."

"I have to say Barry can be quite romantic at times," said Muriel, draining her glass of drink.

"Fancy," said Freda "Would you like another sherry? I'm having one."

"Oh, go on, I'll be a devil and have another. That's quite a nice sherry; did you get it at Mrs Jary's?"

"No, Dick won it in a raffle last Christmas. It's not Harvey's Bristol it just says it's a cream sherry."

"Probably an own brand," said Muriel, "but it is very nice."

"Dick has gone down the Legion tonight; he is being paid to help behind the bar, and I just hope he doesn't drink it before he is paid it."

"That's one thing I've never had with Barry. He likes a drink, but in moderation. He does let himself go on occasions but is a long way behind your Dick."

"Fancy," said Freda, handing Muriel her glass. "I'll see if I've got any nuts left over from Christmas, I feel quite peckish."

Mona Buckle

Mona Buckle and her husband Bertie hadn't got along with each other for many years. It had started when the last of the three children had left home, the two boys joining the forces - William the Royal Navy, Gordon the Merchant Navy - and the girl, Wilma, named after Bertie's late mother, running off with a travelling salesman from Leeds, never to be heard of again. The odd card from the boys dropped through the letterbox, but they had never returned home. However, they both loved their father and every now and then a small deposit was made into his bank account and their mother was none the wiser. Mona had never been maternal, very much following in her own mother's footsteps.

Bertie had his own bedroom with his own lock and Mona was never allowed entry. Although they were civil to each other and Mona always put food on the table, they were hardly bosom buddies and, as Bertie often recalled, his own mother's words were truer now than they had ever been. "Marry in haste and repent at your leisure".

Bertie had always worked, his wage packet was handed over to Mona every Friday and he was given what he described as 'pocket money'. Bertie's bank balance was now looking very healthy indeed, thanks to his sons, and he had made a decision concerning his future. He was going to leave Mona.

One afternoon while Mona was out cleaning, he packed a small suitcase and left his bedroom key on the kitchen table with a note for Mona. Some weeks previously with the help of two

19

friends he had located the whereabouts of Wilma and she had offered her father the use of the spare bedroom until such times as he got on his feet again. He had written to Gordon and William to let them know what was happening and in readiness of his escape, he had secretly parcelled up a few belongings and posted them on to Wilma.

His friend Eddie had offered to drive Bertie to Leeds and met Bertie near the Jetty. As the car headed out of town, Bertie gave Great Yarmouth one last look, feeling that he had made the right decision and he hoped that he would now be able to start a new life for himself.

Mona had picked up some chops from the butcher on her way home and entering the back door of the house, put her shopping basket on the kitchen table. She caught sight of the note and the key and picked them up. She read the few words Bertie had written, signed off with just his initial and sat down at the table. She didn't move for a good ten minutes, then hauling herself up, she took off her coat and hat and hung them on the hallstand. She went to the front door to see if there had been any post and there on the mat was another envelope containing the keys to the house.

Walking slowly back to the kitchen, Mona experienced a sharp pain across her forehead. Never one for headaches, it alarmed her. She got a glass of water and swallowed a couple of aspirin that she kept for Bertie. She turned the gas on under the kettle and prepared the teapot, two cups and two saucers. Taking a bottle of milk from the fridge, she filled the small cream jug and set them on the table.

She put her shopping away, poured the boiling water onto the tealeaves and sat down at the table again.

She poured some milk into both cups, one with slightly more milk for her and less for Bertie. She placed the tea strainer above the cups simultaneously and putting two teaspoons of sugar slid Bertie's cup and saucer across the table.

She sipped her tea, the only sound she could hear was the ticking of the mantle clock, it was coming up for 5:30 and Bertie would be coming through the door any minute now. Mona sat with her tea as the clock ticked, the ticking seemed louder than usual but Mona wasn't bothered by it. The big hand reached the twelve and Mona looked at her tea which was now cold. She glanced across the table to the other cup and saucer and it slowly dawned on her that Bertie was never coming home again.

Mona had a fitful night; so many things kept going through her mind. She looked at the bedside clock and at 3am decided to go and make a drink. The tea pot, cups and saucers were still on the kitchen table and Mona chided herself for not putting everything away.

The kettle boiled and she made a small pot of tea and took two digestive biscuits from the barrel. She slowly made her way back up the stairs and got back into bed. Turning on the bedside light, she drank her tea and ate the biscuits. When she eventually settled down, she fell into a deep sleep.

She awoke the next morning to the sound of the telephone ringing in the hallway. She heaved herself out of bed and waddled down the stairs, feeling bleary-eyed and a little unsteady on her feet. She picked up the receiver and heard the voice of Rita Ricer.

"Hello Mona is everything alright. I noticed you hadn't been to the office as usual this morning."

"I am very sorry Mrs Ricer, but I don't feel very well."

"Oh, Mona I am very sorry to hear that, is there anything I can do for you?"

"That is very kind of you," said Mona feeling a lump in her throat. "I expect I shall be okay after a day of rest."

Rita was concerned, it was most unlike Mona to be unwell and references proved that Mona had never taken a sick day in her working life.

"Look, if you are not feeling well enough tomorrow, please don't come in to work. If there is anything you need, give the office a call and we'll arrange it. Perhaps you should make an appointment to see your doctor."

Mona thanked Rita and replaced the receiver. As she made her way toward the staircase Mona caught sight of Bertie's cap hanging on the hallstand. She sat down on the stairs and cried her eyes out.

When Beverley arrived at the office, she popped her head round the door. "Rita have you got a minute?"

"Yes of course Bev, come on in, I was just going over some wedding details."

Beverley sat down. "I don't like telling tales out of school, but my Ian has heard from a friend of his who goes fishing with Mona's husband Bertie, it seems Bertie has left her."

"That explains a lot," said Rita. "I have just been speaking to her on the phone and she said she wasn't very well."

"According to Ian's source, Bertie and Mona didn't get along terribly well, although they seemed okay at the New Year's do."

"Looks can be deceptive," said Rita. "I have heard rumours in the past about their relationship. Mona always keeps herself to herself; she gives very little away."

Beverley stood up to leave. "I can't help feeling sorry for her in a way."

"I am sure that there are two sides to the story, but that is for Mona and her husband to know and not for us to speculate on."

Beverley smiled. "I'll go and make a pot of tea, I think I heard Jenny's voice."

"Not a word of this to anyone Beverley, I wouldn't want anything that was said in this office getting back to Mona."

"No, of course not," Beverley replied and left the office.

For landladies and neighbours Freda and Muriel, regardless of season, Wednesday was market day in Great Yarmouth and it had been an ongoing arrangement that they went shopping together, Muriel to buy fresh vegetables, Freda as like as not to buy a bit of everything which usually included another pungent aftershave or perfume from a man who sold everything from a suitcase. Freda had become one of his regular customers and it had often been hinted that he was rather sweet on Freda.

However, it was now a good few Wednesdays on the trot that Freda had been absent from the regular trip and she gave no explanation for it, other than she had another appointment. Muriel, who wasn't one to become alarmed, had secretly began to worry that Freda might be unwell, but enquiries seemed to knock that idea on the head, Freda's husband, Dick, could shed no light on the situation and Freda remained unusually silent, so Muriel continued to shop on her own and when asked where her friend was by several other regular shoppers, could give no honest answer.

Freda was hiding a secret. For many months she had been putting away some money and had embarked on taking driving lessons. To ensure that no one was any the wiser she had enrolled with an instructor who was based in Gorleston and every Wednesday she would rise from her bed early, have some breakfast and, once suitably washed and dressed, would hurry off to the town centre to catch a bus to Gorleston. Once there she was met by Larry of Larry's Learners on the Lowestoft Road railway bridge and so began her lessons.

Freda, who listened to everything Larry told her was quite confident from the off. She mastered the gear stick and quite impressed Larry with her three-point-turns and reversing. Freda had never been much good at anything, so it was with some pride that she found she was fast becoming a confident driver behind the wheel after one or two errors with the handbrake and changing gear. Larry would ask her to pull in to a side road to give her some more instructions and Freda would carry them out to the letter. There were one or two hiccups along the way but all in all Freda was doing great.

Following the seventh lesson, Larry proposed to put in for Freda's driving test, so he booked a couple of extra lessons that would enable Freda to prepare for her big day. Of course, it was only to be expected that her friends would ask where she had been to on market day and Freda, who wasn't usually that good at keeping a secret, brushed aside any notion that she was either ill or receiving treatment or had a fancy man. Even her husband Dick had no idea what his wife was up to and she couldn't wait until the day she passed her test and she could tell him what a clever girl she had been.

She asked Larry's advice about purchasing a car of her own and he made several suggestions saying that she would be best to start off with a good second-hand vehicle before progressing to anything more elaborate and he said he would be happy to go along to some second-hand car dealers with her to get the best price.

It was a few weeks later that Freda took her test. The examiner was very pleasant but, to Freda's mind, a bit fierce. Her test got off to a shaky start, with a few kangaroo jumps but Freda, determined not to let herself down, pulled into the side of the road and asked if she might start again. The examiner nodded his agreement and off they went. Reversing, three-point turns, emergency stops, Freda mastered it all and at the end of the test was told that she had passed with flying colours. Larry, who had been waiting for her at the test centre was delighted and Freda, who - for once in her life - was quite speechless was taken for a cup of tea and then once she had got used to the idea, was driven back to Great Yarmouth by Larry who took Freda to look at some second-hand cars.

At first Freda was like a child in a toy shop, the colours of the various vehicles being her first priority. Should she have a red one or a blue one? There was a nice green one. But Larry guided her through the process with the help of a salesman and Freda settled on a red mini which didn't have much mileage on the clock, was in reasonably good condition, although a little paintwork would be necessary, and had passed its MOT. Freda made a down-payment thanks to a win on bingo and after doing some careful sums in her head said she would be able to pay for the car in weekly instalments. Going back home, Freda managed to keep her news quiet; she would surprise Dick and her friend Muriel by driving to her front door.

The following Wednesday, Freda asked Muriel to be waiting on her doorstep at 9am, their usual time for setting off to the market; Dick who wasn't working, was also present. They heard the toot of a car horn as a red mini pulled up by the kerb and from it out stepped Freda smiling. "I've passed my driving test!" she beamed.

Muriel's jaw dropped and Dick ran to his wife and gave her a hug. For once in her life, Freda had done something for herself and achieved what many would have said was impossible and she felt very, very proud indeed. Muriel was quite taken aback and congratulated her friend.

"Just think, Muriel," said Freda. "I'll be able to drive us to the shops, what about that?"

But Muriel, being cautious, said that she would let Freda get the feel of the car on her own first before she sat in the passenger seat.

"Well, you could have knocked me down with a feather when I heard the news about Freda and her driving," said Tessa Goode, who ran a stall on the market.

Her friend Una looked at her and just stopped herself from saying out loud, "With your bulk, it would take more than a feather!" so she just smiled and nodded as Tessa weighed out her carrots.

"And a pound of onions please."

Chapter Three – March

"Thank you so much for agreeing to meet me at such short notice," said June Ashby, sitting down in Rita's office.

"I have to say I am curious," Rita replied, moving a pile of résumés from the desk and putting them in a drawer. "I see that the renovations to the pier are coming along and, according to local gossip, you will be opening by the end of May."

June nodded. "The work has been done much quicker than I first anticipated; the two firms that we employed have been working at a cracking pace. The pier structure is quite secure and the theatre is almost completed. The covered walkway, an idea I picked up from you, is now in the final stages, just a few areas that need a lick of paint to tidy them up. It will make such a difference to people visiting the pier. They can walk either side of the covered walkway in the open air, or in the central covered area. It will mean, of course, the theatre can be open all year round and centrally heating the theatre will be a boon."

"I have to say that it has all happened very quickly. There must have been a lot of work to do, structure-wise alone. I suppose that is what we call 'progress' in the modern age." Rita paused a moment, waiting for a reply, but none was forthcoming, so she continued. "So, what are the plans for the forthcoming season?"

"That is why I have come to see you," said June warming to her theme. "I want to open the Golden Sands with a musical and

I have secured the rights to perform *Hello Dolly* for five weeks from the end of July."

"Hello Dolly? That is ambitious," said Rita, her mind swimming with all kinds of thoughts. "It will be great if you can pull it off."

"And I will, with your help, Rita."

"But I don't deal in musicals. If it's variety acts you are after, then I can oblige."

"You do yourself a disservice," said June. "I know how you work and I believe that if I gave you the casting rights to this musical, you would come up with a wonderful cast. Of course, I do have suggestions to make, having seen the lady work, I wondered if Lauren Du Barrie would like to play Dolly Levi?"

Rita whistled. "Well, me old lover, you have certainly knocked the wind out of my sails. Lauren Du Barrie! I don't know if she would be able to carry it off; it is a big part especially in a musical. Her expertise was opera of course, but that has now faded from her repertoire."

"But Rita, you know as well as I do that most artistes play act all the time and I think Lauren would be able to do it. Think about what she is like off-stage in her dressing room, or for that matter think of my late sisters."

"I would rather not think about them if you don't mind," Rita replied, casting her mind back to the season of '69, one memory she would rather forget."

"Sorry, that was rather insensitive of me," said June. "I think you know what I am getting at, from the moment one of these stars gets out of their car to the time they walk on the stage they are presenting an image of how they think the public perceive them. The part of Dolly is, without being unkind, a sort of grand dame and I think Lauren could carry it off with aplomb."

Rita played with her pen and gave the matter some thought. "Lauren isn't booked for this coming summer season," she said. "She wanted to take a break, however this may just convince her otherwise."

"I take it you are her agent now?"

"Oh yes, absolutely. Sadly, Lauren's days of playing the Coliseum or La Scala are long over, though according to the lady it is just that they haven't found the right part for her."

"My point exactly, the lady is play-acting, perfect for the role of Dolly. Do you think she could manage eight performances a week?"

"If she is willing to play ball, Lauren is a true professional, never been known to miss a performance."

"It might be wise to have an understudy for her," said June.

"Lauren, have an understudy? I can tell you now she would hate the idea, but that isn't to say that someone couldn't be ready to step forward if the need arose."

"Someone like you, Rita?" said June with a smile.

Rita shook her head. "Well, maybe." There was a pause before she continued.

"Now the choreography, would you like me to ask Jenny Benjamin and her team to assist?"

"With no disrespect, Rita, I will need to bring in my own choreographer, James Kenton. He has done several productions back in Oz and would bring this production to life. With regard to a director I did wonder if Ray Darnell would be able to do it."

Rita whistled again. "My goodness, June, you are full of surprises. I can approach Ray of course. He will be directing two plays to go in at Brokencliff. I am not sure how he would feel about a musical, especially on this scale."

"Darling, he is a queen, he will jump at the chance," June replied with a laugh. "I appreciate this is a lot to take on board but I really would like you to be involved."

"There is one condition," said Rita.

"Name it."

"I would like to include Jenny in the audition process."

June nodded. "Of course, Rita, I don't see any reason why not. After all, she knows her stuff."

"Let me order some coffee and then we can sketch out some kind of plan."

* * *

When Rita spoke with Jenny and Elsie, they were both very surprised.

"A musical!" exclaimed Jenny. "Very ambitious and not until the end of July."

Rita nodded. "I think they are going to make sure that the theatre and pier are well and truly ready. There will be a lot to do, for one thing they have to employ staff, the likes of Mona Buckle may consider returning if offered, but I don't think Maud will want to. Maud has made the Playhouse box office at Brokencliff her home, and I cannot see Alfred Barton releasing her."

"They won't approach Bob Scott to return as theatre manager, will they?" Elsie added.

"I think they will be looking for new blood all round," said Rita. "Their plans to keep the theatre open all year round are very ambitious, but it might just be the boost the town needs. According to June, they would attract amateur companies a few times a year. She thought they would bring back twice-nightly summer season and maybe stage some classical concert evenings. It all sounds very exciting."

"Indeed it does," Jenny agreed.

"June has asked me to audition the cast with the emphasis on getting Lauren Du Barrie to play Dolly Levi. Jenny, I would like you to be on the audition panel with me."

Jenny smiled. "Happy to help Rita, you know I can just see Lauren as Dolly Levi."

Elsie laughed. "It will certainly be an eye-opener for the audience."

Rita looked at her notes. "There are to be 30 dancers and ensemble and they will be auditioned and choreographed by James Kenton."

Jenny sat up "James Kenton, my goodness, I remember James when he was knee high to a grasshopper. His family moved to Australia when he was about fifteen, he always showed an interest in the dance."

"So you know him?" said Rita.

"I have kept tabs on that boy's progress. He is certainly the right man for the job when it comes to this venture."

Inwardly, Rita heaved a sigh of relief. That was one difficult conversation she wouldn't have to have.

* * *

Lauren Du Barrie

In her Kensington abode, Lauren Du Barrie was resting on her chaise lounge when she heard the telephone ringing. Milly, her personal assistant left preparing some lemon and honey and went to answer it.

"Oh, hello Rita, how are you?"

"Who is it?" Lauren called, removing the slices of cucumber from her eyelids.

"It's Mrs Ricer, I mean Rita, your agent."

"Bring the phone in here dear, I can't get up at the moment."

Milly asked Rita to hold on while she plugged in the extension in the lounge and placed the telephone on the table next to Lauren.

"Rita, darling, how lovely to hear your voice. I have been resting don't you know, that little show I was in at Christmas last, fair took it out of me. But I must stop talking, you were calling to tell me something or ask me something, fire away."

Rita explained the reason for her call, there was a long silence and then she heard Lauren scream, "Milly the smelling salts dear!"

"Are you okay, Lauren?" asked Rita after a few minutes.

"My darling, this is such a thrill, such a shock, are you absolutely positive that June Ashby asked you to ask me if I would play Dolly Levi? It isn't some kind of joke is it, darling?"

"I can assure you that it isn't."

"I'll audition, of course, that is only right. Have they anyone else in mind besides me?"

"That is the strange thing. June only mentioned your name."

"I feel quite emotional. Of course, I shall have to read the script and the score."

"I am having both sent by courier from French's bookshop today, together with the cast recording of the Broadway show to give you an idea."

"I shall have to begin preparing myself, walks in Kensington Gardens, doing my vocal exercises, Milly is just making me some lemon and honey, it's the voice you know."

Well aware of Lauren's ways, Rita acknowledged that she did know. "I will let you know when we will be holding the auditions and they are likely to be in London, so you won't have far to travel Lauren. I shall say goodbye for now and we will speak again soon."

"Goodbye Rita, my darling girl. Milly, can you believe it? June Ashby wants me, me, Lauren Du Barrie to play Dolly Levi for five weeks. Of course, one never saw Mary Martin or Dora Bryan in the West End run, unfortunately, as we were on tour in '65."

Milly handed Lauren the honey and lemon. "It all sounds very exciting and it will make a nice change for you working with a big company again."

Lauren sipped her hot drink. "To think that I shall be head lining the re-opening of the Golden Sands theatre in Great Yarmouth and of course it could lead to a tour. Milly dear, we must keep a listen out for the doorbell, Rita is having a courier bring over a script, score and a Broadway cast recording. We must dust off the stereo so that we can listen to the dulcet tones of Carol Channing and company.

"Dear Carol, we bumped into each other once in Macy's, she was so lovely and if it hadn't been for the fact she had another appointment we would have had coffee together. Do you remember that, Milly? New York, '63, I remember it like it was yesterday. I wonder who my leading man will be, Harve Presnell perhaps or maybe they can get Donald O'Connor?"

As Milly left the lounge she muttered under her breath, "More chance of it being Des O'Connor."

Following a light lunch of grilled tuna and steamed vegetables, the package duly arrived and Lauren was beside herself with excitement. Milly put the long-playing record on the turntable and they both listened as Carol Channing sang, *I Put my Hand in Here* with Lauren holding her hand to her forehead imaging how she would conquer the role.

"We must listen to that again tomorrow," said Lauren when both sides of the record had been played. "I shall now read the script and see what new light I can shed on Dolly the matchmaker."

Milly excused herself and retired to the kitchen where she began making a Victoria sponge for afternoon tea when Lauren's vocal coach, Estelle Marconi, would be joining them. Although July was some months away, Milly knew full well that Lauren lived and breathed every waking moment as if it were a rehearsal.

When Rita approached Ray Darnell about directing Hello Dolly, while he was on one of his many visits to Brokencliff, she was quite surprised by his reaction.

In the lounge of the Beach Croft Hotel he put down his coffee and looked Rita directly in the eye. "My dear lady, I have never been associated with musicals; plays are my forte as you will know. I thought you had invited me to meet you to discuss the two plays I have been preparing for the Brokencliff run, *Up the Garden Path* and *Death in the Scullery*."

"We can discuss those later Ray," said Rita "Right now, I would like to know how you stand with this offer from June Ashby."

Ray lit a cigarette. "I suppose one should say one is flattered." He hesitated. "And you say that James Kenton is to choreograph?"

"Is that a problem?"

"It depends on how far his memory goes back. He and I had an encounter in Sydney many years ago, it was foolish, a bit of fun at the time, but it did leave a bitter aftertaste."

"If you are not keen Ray, I have two other people I can approach, Sam Brett or Frank Groves."

"Not wishing to sound bitchy Rita, but those two are washed up has-beens. Did you ever see Sam's *Moon over France* or Frank's *Student Wife*? Darling, they were quite dreadful and they would ruin *Dolly* and probably the reputation of Miss Du Barrie."

"I did think of directing it myself," said Rita. "But I have quite a busy year with one thing and another. However, not to worry, I am sure I can find someone."

Rita picked up her bag and made to leave. Ray was clearly worried. "Perhaps I am being a tad hasty."

Rita looked at Ray. "If you need time to think about it, I can give you 24 hours. Thanks for coming along Ray, now if you'll excuse me, I have another appointment."

As Rita walked down the steps of the hotel, Ray came running after her. "I will do it, goodness knows why I am putting myself under such pressure, but I will do it."

Rita turned and smiled knowingly. "My late husband Ted always used to say, never kid a kidder. I will have a contract drawn up." And with that Rita walked away leaving Ray somewhat stung and realising there was a lady he shouldn't mess with.

Rita told Jenny and Elsie about the conversation with Ray when she returned to the office.

"I know it is a lot to ask," said Rita, "but June specifically asked for Ray."

"I have a thought," said Jenny. "We could help out with the production of the show at Brokencliff, it is only a matter of slotting the acts in a time frame. The dance routines will be in the bag if I know Jill and Doreen. The plays will be rehearsed in London and, let's face it, they are the same company of players as last year and they are pretty much self-sufficient."

Rita nodded. "You have a point. I will mention it to Ray when I speak to him."

"I don't know what help I can be," said Elsie "but I am happy to pitch in where I can."

The Toasted Teacake

The Toasted Teacake had been a feature of the Brokencliff Parade for many years. It was owned by spinster triplet sisters Ann, Bea and Cissy Brown. Their late parents had both been in the medical profession, Clive Brown a successful surgeon and Dorothy Brown a local GP. The sisters still lived in the large family home, The Lawns, which was a short distance from Owlerton Hall.

The sisters were now in their mid-sixties, they were all of a short slim statue, wore glasses, their once-light-brown hair was now more silver and they dressed identically, making it impossible to tell one from the other unless their initial broaches were spotted on the neck of their pristine white blouses.

They ran a simple operation, offering pots of tea, coffee and soft drinks. Hot snacks consisted of poached egg or beans-on-toast. A tin of beans would serve two and the sisters would fret on opening a tin in case they were unable to sell the other portion. They had offered sardines on toast, but these had been withdrawn as unpopular and another cause for fretting. Their bread supply came from Mathee's, enabling them to offer filled rolls, cheese-and-pickle, ham salad or egg-and-tomato. Mathee's also supplied them with their teacakes and other cake selections, cutting out the need to do any baking of their own unless one of them had the inclination to do so.

The summer months were their most busy and they often remained open until 19:30 when they were sure to catch theatre goers looking for sustenance.

In winter months they opened from 11:30 until 15:30 offering soup of the day and light snacks.

It was rare to see the three sisters working together, with two of them taking it in turns to run the business. It wasn't as if they needed the money, it was just something to keep them busy.

The locals liked the Toasted Teacake as it was a welcoming place to take a light lunch or afternoon tea with friends. The visitors to the small resort also enjoyed the ambience and often had bets to see if they could tell the triplets apart, a bet that no one had ever won.

Ann, Bea and Cissy Brown spent time at home when not at work. All three sisters enjoyed gardening and grew their own vegetables in a large patch at the side of the greenhouse. A small lawn surrounded by flower beds which were a blaze of colour during the spring and summer months, gave the sisters much joy. On the occasional Sunday afternoon following a light lunch the three would don their summer bonnets and sit in the garden, knitting, reading or just simply enjoying the sunshine. They didn't encourage visitors to the house and on the rare occasion that one should turn up unexpectedly, they would ensure their privacy was not encroached upon for longer than 20 minutes, which they considered ample.

They had shown little or no interest in the opposite sex and thus marriage had eluded them for any suitor would soon realise that he was wasting his time.

Invitations were politely refused and anyone that knew the sisters of old simply crossed them off their lists. The one exception was the church; the sisters were happy to provide flowers for the altar and always attended Sunday morning service. However, requests to volunteer at the church were rejected; they really didn't want to be in the company of gossiping do-gooders, as the three commented, and they heard enough gossip in The Toasted Teacake, which later they would discuss among themselves, but never repeat. The three had long-been of the opinion that Reverend George and Joe Dean, who often came into the Toasted Teacake, were more than just friends. They had always found the two to be friendly and although they didn't fully understand the obvious attraction between the two, they accepted it. When Reverend George resigned from the church, the sisters were the first to hear about it and were quite alarmed. The Reverend conducted the kind of services they very much enjoyed and were a reminder of when their parents had taken them to church as girls. Reverend George had been in Brokencliff for a number of years and they didn't like the idea of change and the three had decided that when he did depart, they would find themselves another church at which to worship and take their floral supply with them.

Saturday 17 March

Lucinda Haines went to the door and was surprised to find two of her regular guests, Dinah and George Sergeant smiling.

"Well this is a surprise, come along in to the lounge."

"I said to George, didn't I George, I need to get out of the house while the builders are in. Making a terrible mess, aren't they George, and it gets so you can't call the kitchen your own."

George nodded and smiled at Lucinda.

"I take it you are having some alterations done to your house," Lucinda asked as the pair sat down on the settee.

"I wish we had never started. New bathroom, new kitchen and all of the rooms redecorated. We won some money on the pools and with some savings thought we'd spruce the place up a bit, didn't we George?"

"We did Dinah," said George, pleased he could get a few words in.

"So, I said to George, come on George, let's pack a few things and take ourselves off. The neighbour next door will keep an eye on the works and she has a spare set of keys, and as we drove along we ended up here in Great Yarmouth."

Lucinda smiled. "You'll be wanting somewhere to stay then."

"We wondered if you had a vacancy?" said George before his wife could chip in.

"As it happens, your usual bedroom is free, how long will you be staying?"

"Just a couple of weeks," said Dinah, "till the worst is over at home, if that is okay with you."

"Of course it is," said Lucinda. "I have a couple of gentlemen staying at the moment who are working on the pier. As we are out of season, so to speak, I will give you a reduced rate, how does that sound?"

"That's very kind of you, Lucinda," said Dinah. "I say, George that's very kind of Lucinda, isn't it?"

"It is indeed, Dinah," said George.

"Why don't you bring your things in from the car? I will go and make a pot of tea."

George and Dinah unloaded their car, placed their belongings in the bedroom and joined Lucinda in the lounge.

"I see they are making progress with the Golden Sands," said Dinah. "We noticed the workmen as we came along."

"Yes, thank goodness. Although it will be a while before they reopen for business, I think August was mentioned in the last report we had in the *Mercury*."

"Just in time to catch the end of the season," said George, helping himself to a biscuit.

Lucinda nodded. "Yes, it will be a bit late, but there is every hope the venue will open all year round."

"Did you hear that George? The Sands will open all year round."

George nodded.

"It will be a boost to the area," said Lucinda. "So it could mean some of us in the guest house business will be able to open our doors out of season. I am quite fortunate that I do have a regular influx of work and business men during the winter months. However, we will have to wait and see on that score and with Brokencliff on the up with changes abounding on this corner of the Norfolk coast will be a force to be reckoned with."

There was a pause as they enjoyed their second cup of tea.

"The Queen is opening the New London Bridge today," said George. "It was on the telly last night when Dinah was packing. I often laugh when I remember the Americans buying London Bridge, thinking they had brought Tower Bridge."

"I had forgotten that," said Dinah, looking at her husband, sometimes he could be a font of all knowledge.

"Your hair is looking very nice, Dinah. Have you changed your stylist?" asked Lucinda.

Dinah smiled. "As a matter of fact, I have, though at first I thought she was a bit of a rip-off, her prices were a bit steeper than I am used to, but I have to say she does do a very good job. My old hairdresser gave up her business and retired to Wales, though why she decided on Wales I have no idea, she isn't much of a one for rain, sheep and open spaces. She used to holiday in Majorca according to gossip, didn't she, George? She would return looking the colour of my late gran's old sideboard. I have never thought of holidaying abroad; I don't think it would suit."

"It is not to everyone's taste," Lucinda agreed, "though it seems to be catching on a lot now and we do notice the loss of business in the resort."

"Well let's hope the Sands will turn that around for you," said George.

"I read in the paper this morning that Noel Coward died yesterday" said Lucinda. "He was such a talented man and a great friend of Gertrude Lawrence."

"Oh yes he was," said George. "Dinah and I very much liked that film with Celia Johnson, *Brief Encounter*. Now that was a tear jerker and no mistake."

"It certainly was," agreed Lucinda, wishing she could get on with some housework.

"Come on George, we mustn't keep Lucinda talking all day and while it's dry we should go and take a turn on the prom."

Lucinda began to stack the crockery on the tray and watched as George and Dinah headed for the front door. Her vacuum cleaner beckoned but as she opened the cupboard door where she kept it, she suddenly felt unwell and had to sit down until the feeling passed.

As George and Dinah walked along the promenade, there was a bit of a nip in the air. Everything looked very different. "It seems strange seeing it like this," said Dinah "It looks so drab and it's very quiet."

George nodded. "I expect they work behind the scenes sprucing things up. The flower beds and grass need time to recover."

They walked as far as the Pleasure Beach and then turned around again. "I've often thought I might like to live beside the sea."

"Have you George? That's the first time I've ever heard you say that."

George smiled to himself, the fact was he had said it before, but Dinah, in her funny way, had never listened.

"I say George," said Dinah. "We could catch a bus and go over to Gorleston and have a look round, do you fancy it?"

"Well, it would make a bit of a change," said George. "Let's go and have some chips on the market and then we can catch a bus from outside the Regal."

"That's a good idea, George, I quite fancy a bag of chips."

Regent Road was deadly quiet, but a couple of the eateries had opened their doors. All of the gift shops were closed, but there were still items in their windows that could be seen through the wire-mesh coverings.

They reached the market place and joined the queue at the chip stall. The town seemed quite busy with locals going about their business.

They doused their chips in salt and vinegar and found a spot where they could eat them without getting in the way of others.

They decided to take the bus that would drop them opposite Gorleston Pier so that they could walk along the promenade by the breakwater. There were one or two people walking dogs and a road sweeper cleaning out the shelters that ran along the back of the swimming pool and Ocean Rooms. The parade of shops that ran beneath the grounds of the Cliff Hotel was closed but the Bingo was open and there were one or two chancing their luck.

"I say, come on George, let's have a couple of games. You never know, we might win a prize."

George followed his wife into the Bingo arcade and found two seats. Ten games later they had both had three wins between them. Dinah put the vouchers in her bag and said they would keep until they came again in the summer, when they might have another stroke of luck and be able to get a prize worth having.

When they arrived back at Lucinda's, she had prepared an evening meal of minestrone soup, roast pork with stuffing, roast potatoes and vegetables followed by an apple pie and custard.

Lucinda took them a pot of tea in the lounge afterwards and returned to the kitchen to do the washing-up. A little bit of extra, out-of-season business always boosted the bank balance and shopping at Murdell and Pocock was paying dividends. The minestrone soup was of the dried packet variety, the roast pork and stuffing had been a boil-in-the-bag, the apple pie was from their best frozen dessert range and the custard was ready made in a tin and only required heating through. She had roasted fresh potatoes and prepared fresh vegetables she had purchased from the market. She checked the freezer to ensure that she had enough meals to cover George and Dinah's stay and thought that a trip to the cash-and-carry wouldn't go amiss and planned to do that the following day.

George and Dinah took themselves off to the cinema in the evening to see *The Greatest Show on Earth* which was on at Cinema One (once known as The Royal Aquarium). It was a film they had seen many years before and seeing it on the big screen again they thought was a real treat. They noticed that the following evening they would be showing *The Great Escape* and the night after *A Countess from Hong Kong* would be on the bill. They decided that the cinema would be their home in the evenings and it would round off days of sightseeing and walking.

Chapter Four – April

Owlerton Hall

At Owlerton Hall in Brokencliff, Lady Samantha and Sir Harold Hunter were finishing their breakfast.

"Harold dear, I've had an idea."

Sir Harold snorted and continued to study his *Racing Post*.

"Harold, don't snort like that, it is not becoming. I have something I wish to discuss with you, a way of bringing in extra revenue."

At the sound of money, Sir Harold laid his paper to one side and beamed at his wife. "Tell me all about it Samie."

"I do wish you wouldn't call me Samie, I don't want the servants hearing."

"But there is no one here; you have given Penge the day off." Penge was their butler.

"And Mrs Yates is way down in the kitchen so she will hardly be in earshot."

Lady Samantha shrugged her shoulders and decided to let the matter drop.

"Now that we have the garden back to its former glory, I thought it might be a nice idea to introduce falconry displays one or two weeks during the summer season and also hold a summer fête, it would all add up to much needed revenue coming in."

"But Sam... Samantha it will cost the earth to have such a display and a fête would take a lot of organising."

"I have been having a chat with one of the managers over at Kessingland Wildlife Park and he said that they would be happy to put on falconry displays in exchange for having the use of the main hall for a staff event; they would look after themselves and clear up any mess. The fête could be put in the hands of our volunteers, they are always willing to put their backs into a new venture, what do you think?"

Sir Harold drank a last mouthful of tea. "Well, you seem to have done your homework. How would we advertise it? It all costs money, you know."

"We would have some posters and handouts made and these could be distributed through the landladies and theatres. I have an acquaintance in the printing business over in Lowestoft who would do a couple of thousand fliers and a hundred posters for a song. You remember Archie Greenwood, you did him a favour entertaining some of his friends at the golf club and I happen to know he is a bit sweet on me."

Sir Harold frowned. "I say, steady on old gal, we don't want any scandal."

Lady Samantha laughed. "Oh, Harold dear, you have nothing to worry about on that score, he just likes to flirt a little, sees himself as something of a ladies' man."

"Oh yes, I remember Archie, had a full head of hair until three years ago, now he wears one of those hair pieces, he looks ridiculous."

"Don't be unkind Harold. Now you go and get yourself ready, we have an appointment with our bank manager and I don't want us to be late. You will have to drive, as poor old Penge is at the funeral of a friend today."

Sir Harold stood up, "Right you are, Samie. I will go and get ready right now, and I hope Penge remembered to polish my shoes."

Lady Samantha smiled to herself; how on earth her husband had managed to get through army life she hadn't the faintest.

Sir Harold had not driven for some time and it showed; his wife was becoming exceedingly worried. "Harold dear, you really need to move over to the left, you are driving down the centre of the road."

Harold snorted as a car hooted behind and he swerved to get back into the proper lane. Lady Samantha winced. "I think I best drive us home after our appointment or we will never arrive in one piece."

"Don't take on so, Samie old gal; I'm just a little bit rusty."

"If it were that easy I could put some 3-in-One on you."

They arrived in Lowestoft and after he had managed to park, Sir Harold opened the car door for his wife. "Here we are darling and we have five minutes to spare."

Locking the car doors, Sir Harold followed Lady Samantha to Lloyds Bank where they were greeted by the receptionist who informed them that Mr Wright would be with them shortly.

Lady Samantha removed her gloves and took a seat. "Harold dear, your hat."

Sir Harold huffed, took off his hat and sat down beside his wife. "Why we both need to be here is beyond me, you'd think we were asking for millions."

"Harold you know as well as I do, that putting our plans into action requires some extra capital. Once things are up and running we will be able to repay our small loan and things will be ship-shape once more. I wanted you here because it is high-time you started to take more interest in our estate. I have enough to deal with on a day-to-day basis as it is."

Sir Harold snorted. "I thought that was why we employed servants, the place should run itself."

"That's all very well, but sometimes things don't happen in the way we envisage."

They were interrupted by Mr Wright who was smartly turned out in a dark grey suit, highly polished brogues and a pristine white shirt with a light-grey tie. He was a handsome man, whose crystal-blue eyes always fascinated Lady Samantha. He was clean-shaven, his dark hair parted to one side and he had a faint smell of Aramis aftershave about him, which happened to be Lady Samantha's favourite. She had long tried to get Sir Harold using it, but he preferred his Imperial Cologne, which his wife secretly thought made him smell musty.

"Lady Hunter, Sir Harold, delighted to see you both," said Mr Wright, holding out his hand to greet them. "Come along to the office, I expect you would like some coffee." He turned to Miss Cain at reception and she smiled acknowledging the request.

"Please sit down," said Mr Wright, holding a chair for Lady Samantha. "I have been reading through your proposal for some extra activities at Owlerton Hall and it all sounds rather splendid."

Sir Harold gave a sharp look at his wife who was smiling at Mr Wright, dagnabbit, she had been working on this behind his back.

Mr Wright shuffled some papers as he sat down behind his desk. "These costs seem very reasonable and I don't think you will need to borrow a vast amount; however, I would err on the side of caution and take out a little bit more just in case you run into any unexpected expenses."

There was a knock on the door and Miss Cain came in with a tray of coffee and biscuits. Sir Harold eyed the tray, oh good there were custard creams and if he wasn't mistaken a couple of jammy dodgers, capital.

"It will just be a question of some cages being made and display perches for the birds of prey we will exhibit. Kessingland have been quite marvellous and it would attract more visitors to the hall and of course open up opportunities for Kessingland."

Mr Wight smiled. "Couldn't Kessingland provide you with the necessary cages?"

"Well they could, but we would like this to remain a permanent feature and if the initial window we envisage is a success we could open it up to others, but the first option would always be Kessingland. I believe we must work with local businesses; it is something very close to my heart. Good relationships with anyone in the tourist trade are all to the good, everyone benefits."

"Quite so," said Mr Wright pouring coffee for each of them. "There is milk or cream and please help yourself to a biscuit."

Sir Harold didn't need asking twice, whipped two custard creams from the plate and poured cream into his coffee. Lady Samantha was about to say something, but thought better of it.

"How long do you think our request will take?" asked Sir Harold swallowing his biscuits and feeling tempted to take another.

"A matter of days, I will draw up the necessary agreement and if you are both in approval and sign the documents the money will be in your business account within days."

"Well that all sounds good," smiled Lady Samantha, "and when our display is up and running you must come along with your wife and see it for yourself."

Mr Wright nodded. "That would be most acceptable, thank you."

"I suppose we could manage a discounted entry fee for you," said Sir Harold who received a sideways kick from his wife.

"There will be no charge Mr Wright, you will be our guests."

Sir Harold snorted and took two more biscuits, if Wright was having a freebie, he was going to make free with the biscuits.

"Some more coffee perhaps, Sir Harold? And what about your Ladyship?"

Sir Harold pushed his cup and saucer forward. "And if you have any more of those biscuits, I wouldn't say no."

"Forgive my husband Mr Wright," said Lady Samantha, declining a second cup. "You would think he never got fed. Our Mrs Yates makes her own biscuits, but I have to keep an eye on Sir Harold's diet, he has a very sweet tooth."

"My wife is the same," said Mr Wright. "She can't pass up on a cream cake or biscuit."

"A bit of a big lass, eh what?" said Sir Harold.

"Harold really, please don't answer that question Mr Wright. Harold, apologise for your indiscretion."

"No need, no need at all. As a matter of fact, my wife is a member of a slimming club; she has always had problems with her weight."

There was a silence, only broken by the sound of Lady Samantha's handbag being snapped shut. "Now come along

Harold dear, I want to pop into Tuttle's while we're here and look at some bed linen. Thank you so much for your time Mr Wright, you have been most hospitable."

"Delighted to be of assistance," said Mr Wright showing the pair to the door.

"Of course he's delighted, that meeting will be on his bill you see if I am not right" said Sir Harold.

"Harold dear, do stop your mithering, now we'll pop into Tuttle's, have a quick turn on the pier and have some lunch in The Claremont."

'Oh good,' thought Sir Harold, he liked the sound of that, if his wife was driving home, he'd be able to enjoy a couple of snifters.

* * *

A few days later, Selwyn Woods or 'Chippy' as he was known in the trade arrived at Owlerton Hall and was shown into the library by Penge, the butler. Lady Samantha walked into the room and greeted her guest. "Thank you so much for taking the time to come along and see me."

Chippy, who was sucking on his pipe, nodded.

"You must be wondering why I have asked you to come and see me Mr Woods."

Selwyn nodded. "I suspect you have a little job that needs doing, your ladyship."

"You see, we are branching out, so to speak. We will be taking a display of birds-of-prey for part of our summer season and we will need some cages made to house them. I understand from my contact at Kessingland that we will have owls, eagles, peregrines and hawks."

"I'm familiar with their cage arrangements. I did some work for Kessingland a while back. You will want a cage for each and some stand-alone perches the birds can be exhibited on beside their keeper so the public can see them close up."

"Well Mr Woods, your knowledge is far superior to my own. Let's go to the garden and I will show where we think the display should be mounted. Perhaps you will be able to give me an estimate for the work and we can take it from there."

Chippy followed her ladyship and looked at the area she had in mind. He sucked on his pipe, took a pencil from behind his ears and, on an old envelope he had in his pocket, began to scribble some notes.

"If you will take my advice my ladyship, the cages would be better over there." He indicated with his left hand. "You see if you have them here, they will be too close to the main building and the birds like a bit of a vista. The perches would need to be near the cages on a small platform which will involve removing a small part of the lawn there."

Lady Samantha smiled. "Yes, I see what you are saying."

"Fortunately, I have some wood left over from a previous job so I could let you have that at cost. It shouldn't take me and young Eric a couple of days to sort this out for you and we could start as early as next week. I've had a cancellation, see."

"And what do you think the cost will be?"

Selwyn scribbled some more notes and handed the envelope to her; she looked at the calculation and without flinching gave Selwyn one of her warmest smiles. "Well that seems to be quite in order, Mr Woods. Can I offer you some refreshment? I know my cook has made some sausage rolls this morning and I am sure she can provide a cup of tea."

Chippy smiled. "That would be most welcome. I've gone without my elevenses this morning due to the missus being a bit under the weather and not packing my usual."

Penge appeared as if from nowhere.

"I do hope your wife feels better soon. Penge, take Mr Woods along to the kitchen to Mrs Yates. I will pick a small posy of flowers from the garden that you can take home to Mrs Woods, Penge will bring them to you in due course."

"That be very kind of you, she will appreciate some flowers," said Chippy, following Penge. Lady Samantha went off to retrieve her secateurs from the greenhouse and her trusty trug.

Once she had picked some flowers and wrapped them in some fine tissue paper that she had to hand, she sent them off with Penge to take to Mr Woods, who was enjoying a fine old natter with Mrs Yates over a cup of coffee and a couple of warm sausage rolls.

The weather was fine and the sun had come through a cloud, so she took her light jacket and decided to have a stroll down to the cliff top which she rarely did. As she walked by The Toasted Teacake, she saw Joe Dean coming out of his caravan park, Finnegan's Wake, she waved at him and he walked across the road to greet her. Joe had only met Lady Samantha a couple of times and felt a little unsure of his self in her presence.

She greeted him warmly. "Mr Dean, how lovely to see you, I don't often get down this end and I can see you have had some wonderful work done to your little park, I see the caravans have gone."

Joe smiled. "Yes, they have all been replaced with twelve mobile homes, least that's what they are known as. They are in fact, static, and all have their own water supply, heating and bathroom and also there are fifteen purpose-built chalets which have a wooden rise around them, giving them an outside sitting space."

"That sounds most exciting," said Lady Samantha "You will be expecting a busy season."

"I hope so," said Joe. "I've taken out advertisements in some trade papers. Would you like to see one of the homes?"

Quite taken by his Irish charm, Lady Samantha went with Joe to the park. He opened up the first static home and she went inside. "My goodness, it is like a palace in here. Did you choose the decor?"

Joe laughed. "Oh no, I left that to the designer. All of the homes are very individual, but along the same lines as this one. The seating area can be made over to an extra bed if needed."

"I had no idea they could be so charming. I've never actually been in a caravan, or dare I say even a cart."

Joe supressed a laugh, then took her ladyship into one of the chalets.

"The bathroom in here is quite spacious and as you can see the kitchen is fully equipped."

Lady Samantha was quite taken by the whole thing. "Why, it even has a separate bedroom. Your guests are going to be well looked-after, I can see. I wonder if you would like me to mention the park in one of my magazine interviews, I am due to do one for *The Lady* next month as I will be promoting our new attraction, a display of birds-of-prey with flying demonstrations and the more people we can attract to the area, so much the better. I am sure that Mr Barton at the hotel will be able to put some business your way too."

"Thank you very much, Lady Hunter, I do appreciate it," said Joe. "Perhaps you could let me have some fliers for Owlerton Hall and I can put them in the vans along with the brochures for other attractions I like my guests to know about."

"That would be splendid," said Lady Samantha. "Once the new batch arrives from the printers I will have Penge bring you some down. It has been such a joy and thank you for showing me around."

Joe Dean watched as Lady Samantha left the park heading for the clifftop. He looked around him and smiled, feeling very pleased with what had been achieved in his little kingdom.

Lady Samantha continued her walk along the promenade passing The Little Playhouse which she noticed was advertising their forthcoming summer bill. Walking further along she was tempted to go in to The Beach Croft Hotel for a light lunch but instead turned on her heels and went in The Toasted Teacake to see exactly what they offered as she had never been there before. Unusually the triplets, Ann, Bea and Cissy Brown were all on duty and being faced with three identical faces fazed Lady Samantha a little.

"Does one sit down?" she enquired, not knowing what was expected of her.

Cissy came out from behind the counter. "Perhaps you would like this table by the window; it has a lovely view of the cliff."

Lady Samantha acknowledged Cissy and sat down. Cissy handed her a menu. "As you can see, we do a selection of light snacks, an assortment of cakes and pastries and pots of tea or coffee."

"Thank you my dear," said Lady Samantha, looking at her watch. "I think I will have beans on toast with a lightly poached egg if I may, a pot of your finest tea and maybe a small fancy to follow."

Cissy smiled and headed back to the counter.

"She would want beans," said Ann with a sniff. "I'll have to open another tin. I hope we will be able to shift the remainder, we don't want them hanging around for days."

Bea looked at her sister. "That's Lady Hunter you are talking about."

"And how do you know that?" asked Ann. "Since when have you been hobnobbing with the gentry?"

Cissy sighed, Ann had one of her heads and she always played up. "Ann dear, why don't you go back home and put your feet up, I can take care of the order. Bea and I will manage just fine."

Ann didn't need telling twice and, taking her jacket and bag, she bid her sisters a good day and headed off home; she hated feeling under the weather.

Lady Samantha felt she was on a kind of adventure. It was rare that she viewed Brokencliff in this way it was usually from the window of her car driven by Penge. Sir Harold had gone over to Acle to see some friends and with Mrs Yates doing her weekly bake it was nice to be out of Owlerton Hall doing something different. She savoured her beans and egg on toast; there was an art to poaching an egg she always thought. The tea was refreshing and the small cake, which was a lightly iced sponge, was quite more-ish.

Cissy was attentive and asked if everything was okay and Lady Samantha, not usually one for small talk, found herself chatting away about all kinds of things.

"Do you get very busy in here?" Lady Samantha enquired.

"Indeed we do!" replied Cissy. "That is why my sisters and I take it in turns to be on duty. "Gives us all a bit of a break, I don't think I've ever seen you in here before, you are Lady Hunter from the Hall, aren't you?"

Lady Samantha smiled. "One chides oneself for not getting out into the community as often as one should and I have to say this little bistro is a haven of delight, I will definitely come in again. And, of course, you are the daughters of Doctor Dorothy Brown and your father Clive a renowned surgeon. I believe my husband played golf with him once or twice. I knew of them of course, but never had the pleasure of meeting with either of them."

"Yes, Father loved his golf."

"You must come along to the Hall one day, I would be delighted to give you a personal tour. We have lots of exciting things planned for the season. Now I must settle my bill," said Lady Samantha, opening her handbag and taking some money from her purse. "And there's a little something for you."

Cissy thanked her and showed her to the door. "Bye then, do call again."

"So what tip did she give you?" asked Bea.

Cissy laughed. "Five pence, if you please, shall we put it towards a holiday?" and her sister laughed. That was the gentry for you.

Penge had retired to his little cottage in the grounds of Owlerton Hall for a rest. The place had been renovated for him and it meant that he no longer had to have rooms at the top of the main house. It was a pleasant cottage and with the help of Mrs Yates it had been furnished with second-hand furniture from a firm Mrs Yates knew along with some leather chairs from the hall which were not used. At her insistence, Lady Samantha had purchased Penge a new bed and mattress from Palmers. Owlerton Hall kept him busy and with his new responsibilities of managing the staff her ladyship had employed, plus the army of volunteers, he found that he tired more easily. He sat down in his favourite armchair near the living room window and gazed out on the gardens. He was looking forward to all the flower beds blooming again, but the trees which were beginning to bud gave him much pleasure. Within a few minutes his eyes had closed and he had fallen into a gentle sleep with only the sound of a bird singing in the treetops.

* * *

Auditions

James Kenton had already auditioned and chosen his dancers and ensemble by the time Rita and Jenny arrived at the Earl's Court studios some days later. James had asked to sit in on their auditions for the main cast and promised he would not try to influence their decision but had added that they should be able to dance. Rita and Jenny had studied the musical in great detail and had made notes regarding the calibre of artist they would be looking for. Today they were looking for a Minnie and a Cornelius.

Phil Yovell was at the piano to play for the artists. Each had to bring a piano score for a song they were familiar with and they would also be asked to sing a number from *Hello Dolly*.

Jenny had counted 24 hopefuls for the part of Minnie and 30 for the role of Cornelius. It was going to be a long first day and an even longer week ahead.

To break the day up, they decided to alternate the parts so that they didn't end up watching 24 Minnies one after the other. It soon became apparent that some of those that had turned up had not prepared or had an understanding of what they were auditioning for. As Rita commented to Jenny, "Agents need to be sure they are sending the right people for the job."

The following day when a similar audition process for Irene Molloy and Ermengarde was to take place, Rita assembled all 55 hopefuls in the studio and told them in no uncertain terms what they were looking for. Anyone who hadn't sung or danced before should leave along with anyone who was unsure what they auditioning for.

There were mutterings among the ensemble and the group whittled down to just fifteen in total, some were to audition for both parts. During the break for lunch, James commented that he liked the way Rita and Jenny worked and he could see some potential players. Rita thanked him and reminded him of his vow of silence. James left the rehearsal room and wasn't seen again that week.

"That's all we need," said Jenny. "A drama queen!"

"Well, once we have decided who is playing who, it will be out of our hands, me old lover and Jamie boy will have to get on with it, besides he will be working alongside Ray Darnell and he won't be pulling any punches there."

"I wonder how Lauren is doing."

Rita smiled. "I checked in with Milly, who was in the process of making some lemon and honey, she said that Lauren was singing the score like she had been singing it all her life. She has been studying with her vocal coach several times a week and it sounds as if she is really getting into the part."

"I think Lauren Du Barrie may well surprise us all yet," Jenny stated. "It's the voice you know, it's the voice."

* * *

A week later June Ashby had a meeting with Rita and Jenny to discuss their findings and was rather put out concerning James's behaviour. "I might have a word in his ear, he can get a little bit above himself at times and I don't want any friction between him and Ray. I have a lot riding on this production. The re-opening of the Golden Sands has to be a great success."

"Is the theatre finished yet?" asked Jenny. "It would be lovely to see inside."

"Well, there is no time like the present," replied June. "If you ladies would like to accompany me to Marine Parade, I can give you a guided tour of the new jewel in the crown. I think you will both be impressed."

Impressed didn't cover it; Rita and Jenny gasped in awe. The foyer of the theatre had a box office to the right of the entrance and, to the left, a spacious bar simply called The Theatre Bar. Small staircases led to the auditorium but as well as the stalls area, a dress circle accessed by a separate staircase had been provided with 30 rows of seats. At the back of the dress circle there was another small bar and the lighting box room for follow spots. Moving away from the usual red upholstery, all the seats were in a plush royal blue. The walls were an array of theatre posters and caricatures of some of the famous faces that had played the theatre. Rita was very touched to spot one of her late husband Ted Ricer.

The proscenium arch was now much wider and the stage went much further back to allow for larger sets; the fly tower and lighting gantries had been improved. As well as trapdoors, the stage also had a revolve mechanism, which could be lowered below stage level when not required.

The dressing rooms were now all adequately equipped with wash basins, a pull-down bed and beautifully lit dressing tables. Two larger dressing rooms below the stage were for use by dancers and/or orchestra members depending on the production. A large and well-furnished green room had been provided and on the door was a gold plaque "In Memory of Comedian Ted Ricer".

The stage door area had been redesigned and any stage door keeper would be proud to sit behind the desk with its modern appliances.

"It is wonderful," said Rita catching her breath and, as she looked at the plaque dedicated to her late husband, a tear rolled down her cheek.

As Jenny and Rita walked back along the pier beneath the covered walkway, Jenny stopped in her tracks. "Rita, doesn't it strike you as odd that the work has been completed so quickly."

Rita turned to her friend. "I can't say it had crossed my mind."

"Think about it," said Jenny. "There was an enormous amount of work to get done and the fire not only damaged the theatre but also some of the pier structure as well. The weather wasn't on anyone's side this winter and I know there have been days when no workmen have been present on the pier, well not just days, weeks. I hope they didn't cut corners in a rush to get it finished."

Rita tapped Jenny's arm. "You may be over-worrying, Jenny. I am sure the powers-that-be wouldn't allow the pier to open unless it was a hundred per cent safe."

Jenny shook her head. "I hope you are right, Rita, I really hope you are right."

* * *

The Beach Croft Hotel

Minnie Cooper, the Executive Housekeeper of the Beach Croft Hotel had been reviewing the staff. Since the hotel's rebirth, business had almost doubled and the venue was full most weeks, even out of season. Minnie ran a tight ship and expected all of the staff to do what was expected of them and, at her monthly reviews, she touched on things that needed improvement.

Two of the staff were a cause for concern, one a young barman Joey Wilkes who had only been in post for three months and a maid Trudy Bull who, although had come with glowing references, was not cutting muster.

Minnie had spoken of her concerns with the General Manager, Stephen Price and in passing to Alfred Barton when he enquired how things were going on the staff front.

Joey was lacking in experience but brimming with enthusiasm whilst Trudy was lethargic, slow and usually late for work.

Minnie looked across the desk at Joey and smiled. "Joey, firstly I need to tell you that you are a well-liked member of staff, but I realise that you need some help mastering the job." Joey, who liked Minnie, smiled and nodded.

"I have had a word with a friend of mine who runs a small hotel in Norwich and runs an excellent bar. If you are in agreement, I would like to send you to Norwich for a two-week training course which I think will help you enormously. I would have liked the training to have been done here, but I think there are too many distractions and being in another venue will help you concentrate and master the in-depth training I know Denny will provide."

Joey grinned. "Oh, that would be wonderful Miss Cooper, thank you very much."

"You will stay at the Swan and Hoop hotel, meals provided, and Denny will oversee the training personally. His small hotel is one step to be becoming a three-star establishment. Shall we say that you will commence next Monday. I will ask the secretary to arrange travel tickets. The training will be five days and you can come home for the weekend if you wish or stay on in Norwich as you see fit."

Joey thanked Minnie and shaking her hand he left the office floating on cloud nine. Joey hadn't had a great start in life, but now he was on his way to making something of himself and he knew his mother would be proud of him.

Minnie glanced at the second file in front of her and sighed; she went to the door and asked Trudy to come in.

Trudy looked tired for one so young.

"Trudy, how are you finding things here?" Minnie asked gently.

"Alright, I suppose," said Trudy in her usual non-committal way. Enthusiasm wasn't something Trudy had embraced of late.

"I have noticed that you are not on time for shifts," said Minnie calmly, "and it is something that needs to be addressed."

"Yes, I am sorry about that but I haven't been sleeping too well, but I do make up the time at the end of the shift."

"Yes, that has been duly noted. I have observed you on more than one occasion and you walk very slowly, in fact I have never seen anyone walk quite as slowly as you. Is there something I should be aware of?"

Trudy shook her head.

"Trudy, what do you do after your shift, do you go home? I understand you still live at home with Mum and Dad."

"If I am on an early shift I like to go and meet up with some of my old mates in town and then sometimes go to the pictures. If I am on a late then I usually hang out at the Tower nightclub, I like to have a dance."

"And you do this most days?"

Trudy nodded.

"Well that may account for your tiredness."

Trudy flushed. "But I am usually okay after a few strong coffees."

Minnie was concerned. "Trudy, firstly I would like you to consider that going out all the time will not help you working five days a week and the shifts can be difficult to manage. I am going to suggest that one week you do all earlies and the following week lates. Some staff prefer to mix up their shifts, but

I really don't think they suit everyone. Secondly, I think you should make an appointment to see your doctor and just make sure that everything is okay. You do eat properly?"

"Oh yes, I usually eat in the staff restaurant here. Mum isn't much of a cook, you see."

"Let's see what the doctor says, Trudy and then we will review the situation again in a month's time."

"Thank you, Miss Cooper."

Minnie closed the file and sat back in her chair. If she wasn't mistaken, young Trudy was with child.

Caroline Hutton, the Assistant Hotel Manager knocked on the door and entered. "Hello Miss Cooper, how did your chat with Trudy and Joey go?"

Minnie looked up. "Miss Hutton, please be aware that anything I discuss with my staff remains between me and them. If there is anything that management need to know I will, of course, make them aware of it during our weekly meetings."

Caroline Hutton felt her face go red, this wasn't the first time she had spoken out of turn in front of Minnie Cooper. "I am sorry Miss Cooper, it was wrong of me to ask, but I did so out of concern."

"Yes, Miss Hutton I am sure that you did. Now, if you'll excuse me, I have a meeting to go to."

Caroline felt herself bow and closed the door behind her. A couple of the staff who were just going off duty saw Caroline and sniggered.

"She's been Coopered" said one and the other grinned knowingly.

65

"Why do I always manage to put my foot in it with Minnie Cooper?" Caroline asked Stephen, who was pouring some coffee.

"Oh, don't take it to heart. Miss Cooper is a professional, likes things done by the book. She keeps the staff on their toes."

Caroline sighed. "Not to mention the other management."

"Grab yourself a coffee and a bun, you'll feel better," said Stephen, smiling. "Then we will go through the staff accounts."

Feeling a bit brighter, Caroline sat down and took a large bite out of her current bun.

Alfred Barton bumped into Minnie on his daily rounds of the hotel and invited her to join him in his office for a chat and a cup of tea. Minnie, who ran a tight ship, checked her watch, mindful of her appointment and sat down.

"How are things going, Minnie?" asked Alfred passing Minnie a cup and saucer.

"Very well indeed," said Minnie with a smile. "I was thinking of making a suggestion concerning staff rewards."

Alfred looked quizzically at Minnie. "What had you in mind?"

"Oh, nothing that would run to too much expense, but I think it would be a nice idea to recognise good work practises. Perhaps offer an 'employee of the month' award."

"And how do you envisage that working, surely an employee would expect some kind of monetary reward?"

"I was thinking along the lines of a certificate signed by management and perhaps a bottle of wine or maybe a gift voucher, say three pounds. This could be extended and each monthly winner would go forward to the 'employee of the year' award announced at the staff Christmas party."

Alfred took a mouthful of tea and thought for a moment. "I like the idea, Minnie, but perhaps it is something we should run by Stephen and Caroline and get some input from Maureen Roberts, our personnel adviser."

"I will ask Caroline to put it on the next agenda," said Minnie, satisfied with the response. "Now, while I am here, I would like to raise this issue of deep cleaning parts of the hotel that are not currently occupied, in order to keep this establishment to the high standards we pride ourselves on; it is imperative that we keep on top of things."

Alfred nodded. "Yes of course, Minnie. Unless you require my input, I would like to suggest that you liaise with those necessary and work out some kind of timetable, will it require bringing in any outside help?"

"I think we should consider bringing in some extra staff to assist with the task, which will be quite a big one. We need to get it right, Mr Barton and revisit it annually, perhaps during the quieter months after Christmas."

"I agree," said Alfred. "Please bear in mind costs and keep me abreast of any financial decisions required so we can build it into the annual budget."

Minnie rose to leave. "Thank you, Mr Barton, if there isn't anything else I must dash as I am due to meet with the linen supplier."

Alfred stood and smiled as Minnie took her leave. And not for the first time, thought what a gem he had in Minnie Cooper.

As the weekend of Easter arrived, 20th to 23rd April, early holidaymakers were seen in Great Yarmouth, Gorleston and Brokencliff-on-Sea, giving the feeling that summer was only just around the corner. The landladies reported healthy bookings and Easter and Whitsun provided the perfect opportunity to try out new menus. The Great Yarmouth seafront had awoken from its winter slumber and the amusement arcades were alive to the sounds of one-armed bandits and games. Joyland beside the Sands pier was busy with families, a few pony rides were to be had and the crazy-golf course was buzzing. The Pleasure Beach at the end of the Golden Mile was open for business, providing thrills and spills to those who dared chance the bigger and more exciting rides for the older children and adults. The model village had opened for the Easter weekend and many families enjoyed watching the model trains go around the enchanting landscape.

The Waterways at the other end of the Golden Mile had two boats taking trips around the Pleasure Gardens that had been freshly planted for the coming season.

The shops with their array of summer stock were open in Regent Road and a brisk trade was being enjoyed by many of the shopkeepers, keen to make a few extra pennies before the start of the official summer season.

A star-studded variety bill was playing at The ABC Regal for the Easter holiday in a warm-up for the main summer show which would star Val Doonican.

Over in Gorleston-on-Sea, a similar picture unfolded and the seafront was once again geared up for business.

Brokencliff had nothing to offer in the way of amusements or entertainment as Alfred Barton had found it difficult to get a show in at The Little Playhouse for a couple of weeks. However, the hotel and Joe Dean's Finnegan's Caravan Park, now to be called Finnegan's Holiday Park, had secured good bookings. The Toasted Teacake was kept busy and the early summer residents were enjoying a quieter break than could be had in the neighbouring larger resorts.

Lady Samantha gave thought to an idea that opening Owlerton Hall with an attraction the following year would be the way forward. Perhaps an Easter Food Fare and reduced-price tours of the Hall. She made a mental note to discuss this with Sir Harold when the time was right. She knew of his funny ways and how best to approach him.

At the Fisherman's, Roberto and Sadie Casalino were going to have live music on Friday evenings through the season and Sadie had also decided to do some hot food in the evenings which would not encroach of the daytime business at the Toasted Teacake, but would attract those who were theatre-bound and didn't want a big meal.

Everyone hoped that the summer of 1973 would be a great season for them all.

Lucinda had taken a break from her busy day and was walking slowly along the promenade enjoying the weather. It was unusual for her to be out, but she felt that all work and no play made Jack a dull boy. The model village was open for business and she decided to go in. She hadn't been in Merrivale for some time and the boards advertised a couple of new attractions. She ambled along admiring the scenes set out in miniature and smiled as a train thundered along the tracks. It wasn't busy and she managed to go around the gardens without being hindered by others. After what seemed an age, but had actually been a little over three quarters of an hour, she was back outside and walking by the Wellington Pier. She purchased an ice cream and wandered along thinking of all the things she wished she had done with her life. Feeling much refreshed by her little adventure she walked home and began planning that evening's meal for her guests.

Chapter Five – May

The New Golden Sands

S everal days of interviews had taken place to engage a new team to manage the New Golden Sands.

Jamie Dormy, a 40-year-old from a cinema management background was engaged as the General Manager with Cheryl Wong, a local, securing the position as his secretary. Her parents owned a Chinese restaurant in Gorleston.

Maud Bennett had been offered her old position in the box office, but had turned the offer down as she found working at Brokencliff with Barbara more to her liking. Selina White was appointed Box Office Manager with a team of three staff.

Edwin Dawson was to be the Stage Manager, a position long-held by the late Jim Donnell with a team of lighting and stage hands reporting to him.

A fortnight later Mona Buckle was asked to attend an interview and a car was sent to collect her from her home. The interviewing panel had been well briefed on Mona's funny ways. She arrived wearing her black coat and hat, sporting peacock feathers, carrying her trusty galvanised bucket and mop. June Ashby who was on the panel smiled warmly at Mona and did the introductions. Glancing at the clock, the time was now approaching eleven and a tea tray was bought into the office.

"I know how much you enjoy a cup of tea and a bourbon biscuit at this time," June said, "so I have taken the liberty of ordering and I hope you will join us all in a cup of tea and a chat to see how you would feel about returning to the Sands."

Mona was quite taken aback. "Well, that is most kind of you and most acceptable."

"Mrs Buckle, the theatre has undergone a very big change making the auditorium the largest in the area and now includes a dress circle. This would increase the workload considerably. I would like to propose to you that you come back to the Sands as our Executive Housekeeper."

Mona sipped her tea and swallowed her biscuit.

Jamie Dormy stepped in. "You see, Mrs Buckle we need someone we can trust. We plan to employ an outside cleaning firm to take care of the auditorium and bar. As part of your duties, we would like you to look after the offices and the backstage area."

Mona nodded, feeling a sense of pride that she should be asked.

"You will oversee the work of the cleaning company and if you spot anything that isn't up to standard you will report it immediately to me or my secretary and we will follow it up with the firm concerned."

"This might interfere with the work I do for Mrs Ricer," said Mona, her thoughts in a whirl.

"I am sure that Mrs Ricer will understand," said June. "This position would be all-year round and not just seasonal as it was it the past."

"In the old days I reported to the stage manager, Mr Donnell," said Mona, feeling the prick of a tear coming to her left eye.

"We have removed that responsibility away from the stage manager as we think this plan would work better," said Jamie, "but I am sure that Edwin here, would be on hand if you needed some advice."

Edwin smiled at Mona. "Of course, of course, I have been told so much about your good work here Mrs Buckle that it really would put my mind at rest to know we had someone of your calibre on board."

Mona looked at Edwin Dawson. "I see things, Mr Dawson and I can see that you and I would be very happy working together."

"Let's finish our tea," said June, smiling, "and then, Mrs Buckle, we can take you on a tour of the new venue, I think you'll be impressed."

Mona smiled, she would be her own judge of that or her name wasn't Mona Buckle.

As she left the theatre, Mona could be heard singing *The Old Rugged Cross*, a sure sign that whatever had played on her mind before had been forgotten.

Many Yesterdays Ago - Edwin Dawson

"Edwin Dawson, stop running in the corridor" said Miss Ferris looking over the top of her pince-nez.

"Sorry Miss" said Edwin pulling up his shorts which had no belt "I'm late for class."

"And why are you late for class?"

"Because people keep telling me not to run in the corridor," huffed Edwin.

"Which class are you late for?" enquired Miss Ferris, a smile playing on her lips.

"Miss Burley, Miss."

"Explain to Miss Burley that I stopped to have a word with you and apologise for being late."

"Thank you Miss," said Edwin, breaking into a trot.

"And Edwin, no running in the corridor."

"Yes Miss, sorry Miss."

For as many years as she could remember there had been many pupils through the doors of Woods Infant and Junior School. Children from large families who lived in cramped conditions with parents who couldn't cope. There was no room for sentiment but the hope that the education they received would enable them to make their own way in the world.

"Miss Burley, you wanted to see me, how can I help you?" asked Miss Ferris looking up from the registers she had been working on.

"It's about Edwin Dawson, he has been late every day this week and it disrupts the other children."

Miss Ferris smiled. "Well, let's see how we can help him. Please take a seat. I think the best way to tackle this problem would be to make Edwin feel valued, as you know he comes from a large family."

"But so do many of the other pupils," said Miss Burley, "and they aren't late for school."

"There is good parenting and bad parenting; Edwin comes from a family whose parents, for whatever reason, find it hard to cope. Their family are like stepping stones in age range and Edwin gets lost in it all. I know there have been problems with the other siblings' schooling, the reason that Edwin came here and not with the others at Wroughton."

Miss Burley nodded. "He is a good boy really and no trouble in class, he gets along with the others and does try hard at his lessons."

"That is all to the good," Miss Ferris replied. "I think I should ask him to be bell monitor, it would make him feel important and he would have something to aim for."

"But that is usually the duty of the older children."

"Well I suggest we give it a try. Send Edwin along to see me and let me have a little chat with him."

"Yes Miss Ferris, of course."

"We can see if there is any improvement and failing that, a word with his mother might be the next step."

"With eight children, it is no wonder the poor lady cannot cope."

"Indeed," said Miss Ferris. "Please close the door on your way out, Miss Burley and send young Edwin along."

There was a timid knock on the door and a rather worried looking Edwin peered around it at Miss Ferris.

"Come along in, Edwin and have a seat, there is nothing to be afraid of. I have a little job that I hope you will be able to help me with."

Edwin smiled, approached the desk and sat himself down, his legs barely touching the floor. Miss Ferris explained the importance of being punctual and the job of ringing the school bell every morning to ensure that all the pupils were on time for class.

"You would have to make a special effort to get here on time every day Edwin or the school governors will not be pleased."

Edwin nodded. "Thank you Miss, I won't let you down Miss."

"That's settled then, you can start on Monday, come along to my office and collect the bell."

Edwin's face lit up, he was determined that he would take on this important task and make Miss Ferris proud.

Miss Ferris pulled open her desk drawer. "Now Edwin, let's see if this fits, I found it in lost property."

She handed Edwin a leather belt and the young boy hopped off the chair to take it, Miss Ferris watched as Edwin tried to put the belt through the loops on his shorts and beckoned him to come to her so that she could help him.

"Thank you, Miss, very much," said Edwin, delighted with his new belt.

"Off you go to class then," smiled Miss Ferris, "and remember not to run in the corridor."

She watched a very proud Edwin close the office door behind him and reflected that it was the little things that made a difference in people's lives. She hadn't found the belt in lost property it had belonged to her young brother who had died at a similar age to Edwin; he had polio. She sat back in her chair, took a deep breath and returned to the lesson she planned to read at assembly the next morning.

That had been over 20 years ago and now Miss Ferris learned that Edwin Dawson was to become the Stage Manager of the New Golden Sands theatre. She had often taken an interest in her pupils and their progress on leaving education and Edwin had worked as an apprentice with Selwyn 'Chippy' Woods. Now here he was ready to take on a new role in life and she wished with all her heart that he would be a great success.

* * *

"Ted, is that you?" said Rita, looking at her late husband who stood before her in the lounge. "You are supposed to be dead!"

Ted smiled. "Hello Rita, my darling, I've been allowed to come and see you. We are given wishes for behaving ourselves up there you know."

Rita smiled. "You, behave, that will the day, me old lover."

"It's not so bad being dead. I've met up with several old friends who passed; it's quite like old times. I've been keeping a watchful eye on you. You really seem to have found your feet with the agency and the move to Great Yarmouth was just what you needed. I was sorry to learn that Don Stevens has passed, but he isn't on the same plain as me. He will be with the new ones."

Rita felt a shiver go down her spine. "I can't believe that you are really here."

"I can't stay long, but I thought I would take the opportunity to visit. Oh, by the way, Jim and Karen said to say hello."

Rita moved to a chair and sat down. "I had just come down to make some warm milk, I haven't been sleeping too well, I've a lot on my mind."

"Indeed, you have!" Ted replied. "A wedding coming up soon."

"Oh, Ted I hope you don't think…"

"He will be no good to you Rita; he is a wrong one and no mistake. You won't be the first women he has deceived with his suave ways, good looks and easy charm."

"Malcolm is a good person," said Rita. "He cares about me. I will never feel for him what I feel for you, Ted, no one could ever take your place, but Malcolm is kind and thoughtful."

"Oh, yes a lot of women thought that about him, he sweeps them off their feet, takes their money and runs."

"No Ted, you must be wrong."

"Rita my darling I know what I know, when you next see him ask him about Pamela Strong."

"Ted, you are beginning to fade, I can't see you properly."

"My time is up and I must go back."

"Will I see you again?"

"I don't know, Rita, but remember you will always be in my heart. Take care Rita."

The image of Ted faded and Rita was left with an empty room and a feeling of unrest.

* * *

She awoke the next morning and her head felt heavy, she looked at the clock, she had slept well passed her normal time for getting up. The telephone beside the bed began to ring. It was Beverley concerned for her lateness arriving at the office and reminded her she had a meeting scheduled.

Rita got herself washed and dressed, grabbed a quick coffee and headed out of the house, she had never been late in her life and as she pulled out of the driveway, Ted came into her thoughts and she could hear the words he had spoken to her during the night and she felt slightly disturbed by the whole experience.

"I have rescheduled the meeting for tomorrow morning," said Beverley following Rita into her office. "Are you okay Rita, you look dreadful."

A very tearful Rita began to tell Beverley about what had happened the night before.

"I am not an expert on these things," said Beverley, handing Rita a couple of tissues, "but maybe it does mean something."

"I keep telling myself it was just a bad dream, but seeing him again, it seemed so real."

"I wonder if you should have a word with Mona, you know she is a bit psychic."

Rita laughed through her tears. "Mona would have a field day with this one and no mistake."

"I will make you some tea and toast, you just compose yourself, it has been an unsettling experience."

"Thank you, Beverley, you have been a great comfort."

Some hours later, Rita had returned home with a headache and not feeling up to the job in hand, leaving Beverley to take charge.

As she pulled into the drive way, Mona Buckle appeared.

"Mona," said Rita, getting out of the car, "Thank you so much for coming, let's go inside."

Mona waited to be asked to sit down. "Beverley said you were in need and she thought I might be able to help you."

Knowing that it was not the right time by the clock to offer Mona a cup of tea, Rita pulled off her scarf and sat down and slowly began to retell what had happened. Mona listened intently, nodding occasionally.

Rita finished talking and waited.

Mona's eye began to water "You know Mrs Ricer, your husband was a great believer in the great beyond, I knew it from the first time I spoke to him. He had an aura and an aura never lies. Your husband may be departed from this world but is ever-present in the next. I can see that you have been greatly troubled by what you have seen, but you have no cause to be. Mr Ricer came to you out of concern, he has given you some facts you were not aware of and now you must decide the best course of action. I would advise you to ask Mr Farrow about this lady Pamela Strong, it may reveal the answer you are looking for."

"You really think that Ted knows about Malcolm, it seems so unreal."

"For one who sees things, and I see things, Mrs Ricer, I believe Mr Ricer is trying to warn you. Mr Farrow may be a nice gentleman, but if your late husband is right, he may not be all he has claimed to be. When Mr Ricer died, he did so suddenly, he wasn't ready to go and the spirits from the great beyond have allowed him to return for a fleeting moment. In the light of day, it may seem totally unreal, but last night you felt his presence. Mr Ricer was on a mission."

"Can I ask you Mona, have you ever been visited by someone you knew who has passed?"

Mona's eye watered even more. "Yes, Mrs Ricer, my late aunt came to me once and told me where I could find my mother's will. At first, I thought it couldn't be true, but as sure as I am sitting here now, it was where she said it was, in the old flower pot in the shed."

Rita stifled a laugh. "Well that is something, I must say."

"If you need any further help Mrs Ricer I will be more than happy to assist you," said Mona, getting to her feet ready to take her leave. "I'm off to get myself a new mop head."

Rita showed her to the door. "You have been a great help, thank you so much."

Mona walked down the pathway humming *The Old Rugged Cross*, which brought a smile to Rita's face.

Rita went to the kitchen and switched on the kettle thinking of how she could best approach the subject with Malcolm.

* * *

Maud Bennett answered the door bell and was surprised to see Elsie Stevens on the doorstep.

"I hope I haven't called at an inconvenient time," said Elsie, "only I wanted to speak to you and your sister Enid if you are both free."

"Come in Elsie please, Enid is in the lounge, come thorough. We are just having some coffee, I will get you a cup."

"Enid, you remember Elsie," said Maud. "She wants to have a chat with us."

Enid smiled. "Of course I remember Elsie, please sit down. Maud, some coffee for our guest."

Maud saluted her sister.

"The reason for my calling is that I am interested in the shop and flat you currently have on the market."

"Really," said Maud. "I am surprised."

"It's like this, since I lost Don I have been at something of a loose end. Helping out Rita and Jenny has been fine, but I really want to move away from the agency and do something for me."

"What had you in mind?" asked Enid. "The shop did do well selling gifts but it all became too much for me to carry on with, as my sister will concur."

"I thought I could make a go of it selling much the same as you did, but I would need some guidance. The flat would solve my home problem, I have loved living with Rita but I really do need to find somewhere of my own."

"There have been several offers on the property, mostly time wasters, so it still stands empty."

"I would like to see the premises first and if I like what I see, I would be happy to offer you five per cent above the asking price to secure the deal."

"Why on earth would you do that!" exclaimed Enid. "Most people want to offer me less."

"I have been left very comfortably off and I know you have been trying to sell for some time, think of it as a gift."

When they had finished their coffee, Elsie drove them to the shop. Seeing it empty reminded Enid just how spacious it was and with a large stockroom.

"There is a door to the stairs that leads to the flat," said Maud, "but you can gain access from the side of the building, which is what the boys did when they rented it. As you can see, this door is concealed within the stockroom so no one but you would know of its existence."

Elsie liked the flat, it was quite roomy and because it still had some furniture, it felt homely; somewhere she felt she could put down some roots.

They chatted for some time and Enid advised Elsie on the kinds of stock she would need, wishing she hadn't sold off the goods she had had, but she never thought the shop would revert to a gift emporium.

Elsie smiled at the sisters. "I think you can both see that I am quite taken with what I have seen and if you would like to shake on the deal, I would very much like to proceed."

"Well that was a turn up for the books and no mistake," said Maud later. "I wonder how she will manage for staff, she won't be able to do it all on her own."

"I am sure Elsie is more than capable of working that out for herself," said Enid putting a marker in the book she was reading. "I will help her with suppliers and then let her run with it. I don't want to become too involved."

"And nor should you," said Maud. "I did hope that someone might make it into a hairdresser; lots of the ladies I know have been none too happy since The House of Doris closed its doors."

"Let's face facts. Doris Banbury was great in her day, but hair fashions have moved on since the perm and finger wave so many women sported. The new salons are where the young ones want to be, they don't want to emerge with a stiff neck, not helped by too much lacquer and a red mark where the dryer has been. She was right to give up when she did. Mind you, it has led to some trying to do their own at home."

"Which reminds me, I spotted Freda Boggis the other day on the market, let me say she was wearing the most hideous outfit and her hair was a complete mess. Honestly Enid, she looked like an accident with nowhere to happen."

"Her friend Muriel is always nicely turned out."

"Muriel has taste in clothes and rumour has it she now has her hair styled by Mr Adrian, no less."

"Well, she is welcome to him" said Enid "I wouldn't have him anywhere near my Barnet thank you very much, he gives me the creeps. Far too effeminate for my liking and gushes over people too much."

"Some women like that kind of thing, you see it all the time in the theatre."

"Well that's where he belongs, on the stage, preferably on the next one leaving town."

Maud laughed. "I'll go and get fish and chips for dinner, don't fancy cooking."

"A nice bit of skate for me and no salt and vinegar, I prefer to use our own."

Maud picked up her bag. "Yes dear, won't be long. If I get down there quickly there won't be too much of a queue."

* * *

"It will be a new start for me, Rita, you do understand that," said Elsie.

"Of course I do, me old lover and I congratulate you on taking that step. If you need a hand with anything I am sure Jenny and I can muck in.

Relieved that Rita had taken the news so well, Elsie smiled. "Thanks Rita, I will keep that in mind."

Rita chatted with Jenny about Elsie's new project. "I really don't think she has thought this through at all. What does Elsie know about running a shop? The hours will be long and unless she is bringing in enough revenue she won't be able to employ staff."

"Perhaps I will have a word with Elsie. I might be able to help her."

"How are you going to manage that, pray tell?"

"I only act in an advisory capacity where the Dancing School is concerned and of course I pitch in with you when you need me, but I do have times when I am not exactly pushed busy-wise. I could offer to do a few hours a week to give her a break if she would like that."

"Well, when you put it like that," Rita replied, "then it might just work. I don't think Enid or Maud will want much to do with the venture. That is the whole reason Enid gave it up."

"I will take Elsie out for some tea this afternoon and run my idea by her," said Jenny

"Good luck with that," said Rita. "Just don't go signing yourself up for too many things, you're not getting any younger and you need to take things easy."

Jenny laughed. "Hark at the kettle calling the pot black, you're one to talk. If you really are going to marry Malcolm then perhaps you should think about passing the reins to someone else, especially with Bob in place at the London office."

"You're right of course, I will think about it. I have half a mind to train our Beverley to oversee this little lot, she has a head for business, knows what she is doing and doesn't take any nonsense."

Jenny smiled. "I was thinking the very same thing Rita, she does know the business, all those years working alongside Bob and if you arrange some training for her, say sometime at the London office and perhaps send her on a course, then you really would be able to take things at a slower pace."

Rita grinned. "I think I will have a chat with Bev while you go and speak to Elsie, kill two birds with one stone so to speak."

Jenny's chat with Elsie seemed to go well and Elsie was grateful for the suggestion. She wanted to get the shop shipshape first of all and then she said she would sit down with Jenny and work out some kind of working arrangement.

Rita invited Beverley to join her for afternoon tea in her office and had purchased some cakes from Mathee's.

Not getting straight to the point she chatted with Beverley about how things were going and enquired if she was satisfied with her work. When the fire at the Golden Sands pier had occurred, Rita had come to the rescue and offered Beverley a job at her office, even though she already had a secretary-cum-receptionist in place. Bob Scott, who had managed the pier for some years, had taken himself abroad but had returned when Rita had decided to take over Elsie's late husband's office in London, putting Bob in charge with an assistant that had worked with Elsie. It all seemed to have worked out for the best.

Pouring a second cup of tea, Rita put the question to Beverley. "How would you feel about taking over the running of the agency from me?"

Beverley put down her cup and saucer and sat back in her chair. "You're serious, aren't you?"

Rita nodded. "You had so much experience working at the pier theatre and Bob always said what a treasure you were. You have come here and reorganised these offices. Julie did a good job and still does, but you came here with a fresh approach that gave us all the kick up the backside we needed."

"You really think I could do it?"

"My dear Beverley, if I didn't think you were capable we wouldn't be having this conversation. I would like to think that Rita's Angels would survive long after I have gone to meet my maker and besides, with me getting married again I would like to put my feet up more often."

Beverley laughed. "I don't know many wives who are able to do that, but I see your point."

"Of course, you will want to discuss this with Ian first, but that being well, I could send you to London to spend some time at the office with Bob and Norman to learn a few tricks of the trade. Send you out on the road with either myself or Jenny, do some on the job training here and consider any courses you may feel you'd benefit from."

Beverley smiled. "I am sure Ian would agree and I would like to say yes to the offer."

"We can discuss your salary and any entitlements later on. We could promote Julie to your current position as personal assistant and then advertise for someone to replace her as a secretary and receptionist. Having two of you out there has been a great help and with the JB Dancing School, it has all worked rather splendidly."

Rita smiled at Beverley. "Look, take the rest of the afternoon off, go home have a chat with Ian and give me your answer, if you need more time to think things through, by the end of the week."

Beverley shook Rita's hand and left the office on cloud nine.

Rita dialled the number now familiar to her.

"Hello. Mr Farrow's office."

"Hello Linda, it's Mrs Ricer here, is Malcolm there please?"

"I am sorry Mrs Ricer, Mr Farrow is away on business."

'That's strange,' thought Rita. He had not said anything to her when they last spoke, which was a good couple of weeks now, they had both been so busy. "Thanks Linda, I will try him at home this evening."

"Oh, I wouldn't do that," said Linda. "He won't be there and I am not sure of the exact date he is due back."

Rita thanked Linda and replaced the receiver, feeling very puzzled indeed.

Elsie had decided to go over to Lowestoft to have a look around Tuttle's. She was thinking of what she should wear in her shop, nothing too formal and nothing too casual. She tried on several variations, jacket and trousers, skirt and jacket, dress with a smart waistcoat but could not decide what to buy. She thanked the assistant and said she would come back later after having a light snack.

She decided to walk along the High Street and found herself near the Sparrow's Nest, knowing they had a café adjacent to the theatre.

She ordered a pot of tea and a ham roll and sat down near the window. There were a few people in and some taped music could be heard in the background.

She became aware of two ladies sitting near her and although she wasn't one to eavesdrop, her attention was drawn to the ladies when she heard the name of Malcolm Farrow spoken.

"Well, of course it came as rather a surprise and no mistake. My Linda was there when the woman turned up."

"And she said she was looking for Malcolm Farrow?"

"Oh, more than that, she said she was his wife."

"No, I can't believe it."

"Well it's true, my Linda was going over some invoices and the woman who introduced herself as Pamela Farrow. She spoke with a strong Australian accent."

"But isn't he supposed to be marrying that Rita Ricer?"

"Well that looks unlikely given the circumstances."

"You're sure your Linda heard correctly, you don't think the woman might have been his sister?"

"No, I don't. She definitely said 'wife'."

"So, did this Pamela person get to speak to Malcolm?"

"Well that's the funny thing. Malcolm hasn't been seen for a week or more. No one can raise him at his house in Oulton Broad and there is no answer from his telephone."

"What a to-do and no mistake. It's that Mrs Ricer I feel sorry for, such a nice woman, she and Malcolm seem so well-suited."

"Well, there you go Florrie, you never can tell. I wouldn't want to be in his shoes when either his wife or Rita catches up with him. There'll be one or two choice words spoken then or my name's not Alice Rodgers."

Elsie sat dumbfounded. She didn't know what to do for the best. She finished her tea, left a tip for the waitress and headed back down the High Street back to Tuttle's. She attracted the attention of the assistant who had helped her and said she would take all the combinations she had tried on. The assistant was so pleased and knew that some much-needed commission would be coming her way. Elsie wrote a cheque for the purchases and then went to locate her car, which she had parked near the docks.

Stepping on the gas, she headed back to Great Yarmouth. She reached Rita's house and went inside. This had been her home since moving to Great Yarmouth and she would be sorry to leave it as she had enjoyed sharing it with Rita. One of the reasons she had decided upon the shop and flat was so that she had somewhere to live when Rita and Malcolm were married, but after hearing the two ladies talking, that seemed unlikely now. She braced herself. She would have to tell Rita what she had heard.

An hour later, Elsie heard the key in the lock. Rita walked into the lounge where Elsie was sitting. "You have been a busy girl," she said looking at the Tuttle's carrier bags.

Elsie smiled. "Sorry, I meant to take them upstairs."

"Don't worry about that, me old lover. I'll go and put the kettle on and you can tell me all about it."

"All about what?" said Elsie nervously.

"About the purchases you've made, you look as if you have bought half the store. Oh, by the way, Jenny is coming over for her tea tonight. There's that shepherd's pie I made yesterday and we can have some cabbage and carrots with it."

"Yes, that would be very nice," said Elsie.

Rita returned with the tea tray and set about pouring. "Been trying to get hold of Malcolm but that secretary of his, Linda, says he is away on business. Funny that, he never mentioned anything to me. Did I tell you about the dream I had? Funny really now I think of it, but it was like old Ted was actually here."

Elsie sipped her tea. "I don't understand, Ted is dead, how could he be here?"

"Well that's just it, me old lover, he wasn't, it was just a dream, or a spiritual happening, at least that was what Mona Buckle put it down to."

"You spoke to Mona Buckle about it?"

"Well yes I did. It was Beverley's suggestion."

"What was the dream about?" asked Elsie who was now curious to where the conversation was going.

"Daft really, it was old Ted coming to warn me against marrying Malcolm."

Elsie gulped.

"Is there something wrong Elsie, you have gone a deathly white, are you coming down with something?"

"Oh Rita, I don't know how to tell you this."

Just then the doorbell rang and Jenny arrived, bearing flowers and chocolates. "Thought these would be appreciated," she said, handing them to Rita. Rita thanked her and went to get another cup and saucer. "Help yourself to tea, Jenny. Elsie was just about to tell me something."

"It will keep for later" said Elsie.

"Come on, me old lover, spill the beans," said Rita, making herself comfortable in her favourite armchair.

"I went to the Sparrow's Nest café for something to eat," began Elsie, "and I overheard two women talking about Malcolm."

"That reminds me, Rita. A lady came to the office just after you had left, asking for you. Oh blast, I've forgotten the name," said Jenny. "I knew I should have written it down, anyway not to worry she said she would drop by the office tomorrow morning."

Elsie cleared her throat. "Was her name Pamela by any chance?"

"That was it, Pamela, how did you guess?"

It was the turn of Rita to go white. "Pamela, did she say her name was Strong, Pamela Strong?"

"She never gave a surname," said Jenny. "Hey, what is going on here?"

Elsie swallowed hard. "Her name is Pamela Farrow, she is Malcolm's wife."

Rita dropped her cup and saucer and the tea spilled down her dress. "Oh, my dear God, Ted was right, the dream was right. I knew something was up. I haven't heard from Malcolm for weeks now."

"Forgive me for asking, but what has Ted got to do with anything and how do you know, Elsie, that this women is Malcolm's wife?"

Elsie looked at Rita, then at Jenny and back at Rita. "I best fill you in on what I overheard today."

There was silence as Elsie told her story. Jenny watched Rita, worried and upset for her friend. When Elsie had finished there was another silence which was eventually broken by Rita. Her voice was steady and she showed no signs of emotion.

"All my life, there has only been one man I have truly loved and that was my Ted. The old bugger could lead me a dance sometimes, but he was always there for me and me for him. When he died, something died inside of me, but then came strength to carry on in the way Ted would have wanted me to. The other night he came to me in what I can only describe as a dream and he warned me against Malcolm and he mentioned the name Pamela Strong. I ran it by Mona Buckle and she said it was a sign and that I needed to take care. Malcolm swept me off my feet and I was overwhelmed by the attention, he is handsome, debonair, charming and we made each other happy. But I realise that it was all too good to be true and this has proven it. Malcolm Farrow is all the things my Ted was not, but my Ted was not a bastard. Malcolm Farrow wears that title with some pride."

She stopped and her eyes rested on a photograph of Ted, smiling at her, in its silver frame. She got up from the armchair and walked towards the cabinet.

"Would you ladies join me in a large brandy? I could bloody well murder one."

The following morning Beverley knocked on the door and peered at Rita who was, as usual busy, at her desk. "There is a lady called Pamela Farrow here to see you."

Rita winked at Beverley. "Please show her in Beverley and perhaps you could bring in some tea or coffee."

Beverley smiled and returned with Pamela Farrow. Rita stood up and held out her hand, Pamela was dressed in a smart two-piece with a large bow at the neck of her blouse, her blonde hair was cut in a pageboy style and her makeup was minimal.

"I am so very sorry to barge in like this," said Pamela shaking Rita's hand and sitting down.

Rita sat back down behind her desk and pushed the papers she had been working on to one side. "It is no problem, when one is a theatrical agent, you get used to constant interruptions. Now how can I help you Mrs Farrow?"

"There must be some mistake," replied her guest. "I am not Mrs Farrow, I am Malcolm Farrow's sister."

A bead of sweat ran down Rita's face and she felt a shiver go down her spine. "I don't understand, word came to my ear yesterday that you were Malcolm's wife."

Pamela laughed. "Oh dear, someone has got the wrong end of the stick, my late husband Roy will be turning in his grave."

Just then Beverley arrived with a tray of tea and coffee, nodded at Rita and left quickly.

"But my secretary Beverley introduced you as Pamela Farrow, I really don't understand."

"I have reverted to my maiden name. I was, until my husband Roy died two years ago, Mrs Pamela Strong."

Rita, who was attempting to pour some tea, felt her hand begin to shake.

"Here, let me do that, Mrs Ricer," said Pamela reaching out to take control. "I hope you don't mind but I always drink coffee."

"So, what is it that I can do for you?" asked Rita relieved to be free of the elevenses duty.

Pamela passed Rita her tea and then sugared her coffee and sat back in the chair. "I rather think it is what I can do for you Mrs Ricer. Let me explain, every now and then, Malcolm goes missing. He has a personality disorder, you see, and there is no telling what he will get up to. The last time I tracked him down to California, USA. He has a knack of wheedling himself into a job that he is barely qualified for and then usually falling head-over-heels in love with some gullible female. It can be quite distressing for all concerned."

"But how did you come to me?"

"Well, it is my guess, Mrs Ricer - or may I call you Rita? - that Malcolm has proposed marriage to you, am I right?"

Rita nodded. "Unfortunately, Malcolm has married twice before, but has never been divorced. He has a wife in New Zealand and one in the USA."

"So, he is a bigamist?" said Rita trying to get to grips with what she was hearing.

"The thing is he doesn't know he is doing it. After some mighty big detection work on my part I tracked him down to England and, through several leads, here I am in Norfolk. I have since learnt that my brother has supposedly purchased a property in Oulton Broad and has been working at the Sparrow's Nest theatre as a manager."

"Yes, that is correct."

"Well, my dear Rita, he doesn't own the house, he only rents it and it would appear that he has done a midnight flit and disappeared again."

"Are you sure? That really doesn't sound like the Malcolm I know and love."

"When did you last see him or speak to him?"

"We spoke two or three weeks ago on the phone and I admit we haven't seen each other for a number of weeks. I am very busy at the moment and the niceties of life sometimes have to take a back seat."

Pamela drank her coffee and continued. "So, you see I need to find him and try and get him to stand up to his responsibilities, besides when the law catches up with him he is looking at a lengthy stretch in the clink."

Rita began to laugh. "Forgive me, but this all sounds too ridiculous for words, it is like something out of an American soap opera. Peyton Place would kill for this storyline."

Pamela looked at Rita in a kind way, her eyes crinkled at the corners. "You seem like a very nice person Rita and I can see that this is a lot to take in. I should add that I have already informed Scotland Yard of my brother's activities. You see he is a danger to himself and he needs medical help. To put it bluntly my brother is a liar, a cheat and a very sick man. Tell me Rita, have you given him any money, is there any joint bank account."

"Oh no, absolutely nothing, we hadn't even set a date for a wedding, so there has been no financial loss on my part, just a very confused state of mind."

"I hope you are being straight with me, because if any money has changed hands I can reimburse you right here, right now, I came with my cheque book."

Rita poured herself another cup of tea. "I suppose you could say I've had a lucky escape."

"That's one way of looking at it," Pamela replied reaching for the coffee pot. "Believe me the last one was left truly high and dry."

"All I can say is, I have no idea where Malcolm has gone but if you leave me your contact details you will be the first to know if I do hear from him."

"Did you fall in love with Malcolm?"

Rita managed a smile. "Perhaps a little bit, but since the death of my husband Ted, I really didn't get as caught up with it all as I might have if I'd always been single."

Pamela handed Rita a card. "You'll find all my contact details on there and I've written the number of Scotland Yard on the back should you feel the need to contact them. There is also the name of the detective who is looking after the case."

"Have you told them about me?" asked Rita.

"Well I only found out about you a few days ago from that secretary at the Sparrow's Nest, Linda her name is. A bit ditsy if you want my opinion, no doubt it was her who started the rumour about me being Malcolm's wife."

After a few pleasantries, Pamela Farrow took her leave. Beverley looked closely at the lady as she said goodbye and couldn't help thinking that she seemed slightly unhinged.

Rita pulled open her desk drawer, took a couple of aspirin from her emergency supply and swallowed them with some cold tea. She looked over at the shelf and a frame containing a photograph of Ted as it fell over. She put her hands to her face and let the hot tears fall silently.

Jenny knocked on the door. "Rita are you okay?"

Rita looked up and nodded and explained the conversation she had had with Pamela.

"I've been thinking about the dream you had and how you might have remembered the name of Pamela. I have kept cuttings from the newspapers about shows for my scrapbook and I remember that when Malcolm was interviewed by the EDP he mentioned Pamela Strong his sister. I have it here, look."

Rita looked at the cutting. "Well that explains it" she said pulling herself together. "It did seem incredible that I should have dreamt it. I thought I was going mad."

"Think of all the people we come across in our business, names we hear, snatched moments of conversation. We store them in our memory bank and lo-and-behold, they come to us at unexpected moments."

"I am still finding it hard to get my head around it all. I can't believe that Malcolm could be so devious."

"Perhaps his sister has painted it blacker than it actually is. After all, you only have her word for it that what she has told you is true."

Rita nodded. "Yes, that is true, but I don't have the energy to go looking for further answers. Marrying again maybe wasn't to be."

Rita handed over the card that Pamela had given her. Jenny picked up the telephone and dialled the number hand-written as the contact at Scotland Yard.

"Good morning. Could I speak to Detective Julian Brent please? My name is Jenny Benjamin; I am calling about Pamela Farrow/Strong."

"I am sorry, madam, but we have no detective of that name here."

Jenny looked at Rita. "Is there anyone who was dealing with a Pamela Strong or Farrow?"

"I would need to make some enquiries. If you could give me some more information and your contact details, I can get back to you. I am Sergeant York."

Jenny told Sergeant York what she knew and gave him her details and also those of Rita, who was sitting looking at her in astonishment. "Thank you so very much, you have been most helpful."

"What was that all about?"

"Well for starters the information Pamela has written on here is false, no one has heard of this Detective Julian Brent, according to Sergeant York. I really think, Rita, that this has all been a cock-and-bull story."

"So where is Malcolm, then? And why would some woman, claiming to be his sister, come in here to tell me a pack of lies? It makes no sense at all."

"Perhaps we should go to Scotland Yard ourselves and find out what we can," said Jenny.

"I'm not sure," said Rita. "We have little to go on and, besides, it may be best we wait and see what this sergeant comes back with."

"Perhaps you are right," said Jenny. "You know what I am like, see something and want to get to the bottom of it right away. I wonder where this Pamela woman has been staying, if indeed her name is really Pamela."

Rita groaned. "Well, me old lover, I can't go worrying about that now."

A couple of days later Rita received a call from Sergeant York who explained that no person calling herself Pamela Farrow/Strong had made any such visit to the Yard. He said he would put out a call to other stations in case something should crop up and, in any event, get back to her.

Beverley and Julie had kept themselves busy trying to find a cleaner to replace Mona who would be leaving to work at the Sands. It seemed a thankless task. They had placed advertisements in the local press, cards in newsagents' windows and all but resorted to wearing sandwich boards when they went shopping in the town.

It was Jenny who found the solution, a lady she knew who had recently lost her husband and was fed up staying at home might be interested, her name was Harriet Fraser, she was in her mid-fifties. So, one afternoon Harriet was asked to come into the office, Beverley interviewed her and left Julie to show her around the premises pointing out what would need to be done. Harriet was a short lady, well-dressed, sported a hairnet under which Beverley suspected was a perm, she had wide eyes, a small nose and a mouth that gave the impression of a permanent smile. She wore American Tan tights and low-healed leather brogues.

Beverley offered her the same hourly rate that Mona had started on, with a review after six months. It would be sixteen hours a week and she would be given a free hand to work as she thought best. Harriet was delighted to take the position and was introduced to Mona Buckle as a matter of courtesy. Mona was to spend some time with Harriet to show here how she worked.

"If you take my advice, Mrs Fraser, you'll ask for your own galvanised bucket and mop. Do you use one at home?"

"I have to say that I don't, I have a squeegee mop."

Mona was alarmed. "Oh, my goodness, Mrs Fraser! I am surprised to hear that, you'd be better off with a galvanised."

Harriet worked along with Mona a couple of days and thought she would soon get the hang of things.

Mona had given her notice and on her last day she left a parcel for Harriet as a good-luck gift. It was, of course, a galvanised bucket and mop with a good-luck card attached, with regards from Mrs Buckle.

It caused many a mirth-making moment in the offices for some days following.

Not quite knowing what to give Mona as a leaving present from the office staff, they all pooled some money and gave her some Palmers gift vouchers, which they knew she would appreciate, and a bouquet of flowers. Mona was delighted, she had spotted some brushes in the kitchen department at Palmers that she liked the look of.

Elsie busied herself in the shop, she had had the interior painted in lemon and white to brighten the place up and had removed some of the shelving, which she thought had made it look too cluttered. She had decided that she would sell a few souvenir items and seasonal merchandise, but had also decided on old fashioned confectionery, selling sherbet lemons, bonbons, toffees and rock sweets by the quarter. One or two well placed large boxes of chocolates and a few chocolate bars that she favoured. The shop was to be renamed 'The Gift Box' and a yellow-and-white striped awning completed the exterior. Jenny came in to help her and was impressed by what had been done.

"I called in Chippy and his men," said Elsie, "after taking some advice from Alfred Barton. They have also done the flat above. You must go up and have a look while I make us some tea."

Jenny had seen the flat when the boys, Dave and Dan, had rented it for a short time from Enid, before going off to Blackpool to settle down. It had changed completely. There was a lovely fitted kitchen and bathroom, the lounge was nicely carpeted with beautiful drapes at the windows. The furniture was all quite modern and the bedroom was an oasis of charm and comfort.

Elsie gave Jenny her tea. "Well Elsie, Enid won't recognise the place, I cannot wait to hear what she makes of it. It is really lovely and I am sure you will bring in some new business."

"I am taking out advertisements in theatre programmes and also in the local press offering a small discount to customers who spend five pounds or more. I have also got some give-away keyrings advertising the shop."

"When do you plan to open?"

"First week of June, as that's when some of summer shows begin and the advertisements will run throughout the season."

"You must let me know what days you will want me in to help and you will have to explain the cash register to me."

"Oh, that's quite simple, it does all the adding for you, so you won't be writing things down on bits of paper the way Enid used to do. I can show you how to work it now if you'd like once, we've finished our tea."

Jenny nodded. It was good to see Elsie enthusiastic about doing something for herself, as Don's untimely death had come as a blow to her.

"I thought the shop should open at 9:30 and close at 5:30, Monday to Saturday with a half-day closing on a Thursday, in keeping with the general shop hours of the town, although I think through the summer season I will keep open all day Thursday at least until the middle of September anyway. Once you are comfortable with the proceedings I will take one day off during the week and also employ a part-time person with hours to suit, maybe ten hours a week. I have been looking at the pay scales and although I will have to start off with a minimum, once the shop begins to make a profit I will be able to up the hourly rate."

"Until then Elsie, you must consider my help totally free of charge," said Jenny.

"Oh no, you couldn't possibly work for me for nothing," said Elsie, horrified at the thought. "I won't take advantage of you like that."

Jenny grinned. "Look it really will be my pleasure to help out, I do less and less at the Dancing School now and Rita has everything tied up with a neat bow at the agency."

"I do feel sorry for her, over this Malcolm business," said Elsie.

"Yes, she must feel quite hurt," agreed Jenny, finishing her tea. "But Rita is a tough cookie and she will rise above all the nonsense."

"Do you think she will really hand over the reins of the business to Beverley?"

"Yes, I do. I Know Beverley is very keen and once she has learnt the ropes she will always have Bob and Norman in the London office to turn to for help. As you know, Beverley was Bob's secretary for years at the Sands. I think once everything is in place, Rita may well return to live in Hull."

"She wouldn't do that surely, she always said that she and Ted were always happiest when they came to Great Yarmouth, that's one of the reasons she sold the house in Hull."

"Yes, I'd forgotten that, maybe she will just look for something a bit smaller, there are some lovely cottages to be had around about if you know where to look."

Elsie put the cups in the sink. "Now, let me show you how this till works."

* * *

"I see Princess Anne has announced her engagement to Captain Mark Phillips," said Freda reading from the newspaper.

"He looks a very handsome man," said Muriel. "It will be nice to have a Royal Wedding to look forward to."

"Wouldn't it be lovely if they invited us?" said Freda, thinking her old faithful could do with an outing.

"It would be a bloody miracle," said Muriel with a laugh. "Imagine us at a Royal Wedding."

"I can see it now in my mind's eye," said Freda with a sigh. "And apart from the television that is the only place you are going to see it," said Muriel. "Now finish your bath bun and let's be having you."

Chapter Six – June

The studio at Earl's Court was a hub of activity. The Clifftop Players had settled in for a week of rehearsals to bring to life the two plays they would be performing, *Death in the Scullery* and *Up the Garden Path*. It was the same group of players from the previous season and all of them were pleased to be working together again.

Constance Anderson made a point of going around the room followed by her husband William Forbes, shaking hands with everyone. This, in turn, prompted everyone to do likewise. Ray Darnell, the director looked on and wondered whether it would be in order to suggest a coffee break to get the camaraderie out of the way. Everyone quickly settled down and they began a read-through of the plays.

Edith Harris looked up from the script of *Death in the Scullery*. "I have to say, Ray, this plot appears to be all over the place. We are given to believe that a jar of homemade chutney is responsible for the death of one of the staff of Gables Guest House. The character is mentioned but never seen and her last words are noted as being, 'That chutney had a funny twang to it'."

"Quite so," said Ray, "and if you wait until the next scene you will see that the chutney has been supplied by a member of the Women's Institute, the problem being that several jars were donated to the guest house from three different members."

"I have never been a lover of chutney," said Edmund Green, adding his bit to the conversation. "Although I will admit to liking Pan Yan".

"Now if anything has a funny twang, that does," William Forbes added, "and whilst we are on the subject, how come Inspector Cross, who I played last year, is making a comeback in this play that is not written by the same the playwright?"

Ray smiled. "I thought it would be a good idea to revive the Inspector and so in agreement with both playwrights we changed the name to Inspector Cross from what would have been Inspector Rowley Moss."

William sighed. "Imagine being called Rowley Moss. Good move, Mr Director."

"Now if we have no other concerns about chutneys of any sort, I suggest we press on with scene two and then we can break for lunch."

Constance smiled. "I suggest none of us entertains a ploughman's, the pickle may be suspect."

Ray gave Constance a withering look. "Shall we proceed?"

Over lunch at the local watering hole, Constance talked about the re-opening of the Golden Sands. "They are due to open the doors at the end of July. William heard about it from an old friend in Norwich. I think one of the most unusual aspects about the whole thing is that they are going to open with a musical."

"Hello Dolly," added William tucking into his steak and kidney pie. "You'd have thought they would have launched with a twice-nightly variety show."

"Well according to our source, the Australian company that have purchased the pier wanted to do something different. You have all heard of June Ashby, well she is at the forefront of it all," said Constance, playing around with a portion of chutney, not knowing whether to taste it or send it off to be analysed; she had been brave and ordered a ploughman's. "I'm not one for gossip as you know, but they have asked Lauren Du Barrie to play Dolly Levi."

"Well, she was a good singer in her day," said Edith.

"In her day, yes, and let's face it, she can hold a tune." Constance continued with a nod to Edith "but is she really up to a musical of this calibre? I wonder what Jerry Herman would make of it?"

"Well, he's hardly likely to fly over to Great Yarmouth and find out," said Patrick Prowse. "I saw Mary Martin at the Lane and then I was fortunate enough to catch Dora Bryan in the role, they were both marvellous. You never know, Lauren Du Barrie may bring her own magic to the part, look what she did with *Iolanthe*."

"Exactly," said Edith. "It certainly was different, by all accounts."

Julia Burton put her glass of lemon and lime to one side. "I think you are all being terribly mean. I went to see Lauren Du Barrie twice last season and I thought she was jolly good and I have every intention of seeing her in *Dolly*."

William patted her hand. "That's very commendable of you my dear. Perhaps we could all make up a party, trot over to the Sands and judge for ourselves."

"I think that would quite in order," said Edith, "and I am sure Lauren would be pleased to know we had taken the time to go and see her."

Everyone nodded in agreement and Ray said he would have a word with the box office about a date.

"We don't want comps," said Constance. "If we are going, then we will all pay the going rate. That is only fair."

"Spoken like a true pro," said Ray. "I will sort it out."

Constance decided to tackle the chutney with some bread and cheese.

"Everything alright, my sweet?" said William, watching his wife.

"That chutney has got a funny twang," said Constance and, with that, the group started to laugh.

* * *

Lauren is interviewed on BBC Look East

"We are delighted to welcome one of the theatre's best-loved stars, Lauren Du Barrie," said Jane, one of the presenters of Look East who had been assigned the task of interviewing Lauren.

Lauren, who was dressed in a black and red kaftan with matching turban, smiled at the camera.

"So, Lauren you will be starring in *Hello Dolly* when it re-opens the much-loved Golden Sands theatre in Great Yarmouth."

Lauren beamed. "When I got the call asking me to play Dolly Levi, I was beside myself with excitement, I had promised myself some leisure time this summer season, but it seems my public needs me."

"You have played the Golden Sands theatre before?"

"No, I haven't, I was at Brokencliff at the Playhouse. The fire was such a dreadful thing to happen, but one mustn't dwell on what has happened, but look to the future with hope. I have yet to see the new theatre, but I am told it is beyond beautiful. I am very much looking forward to acquainting myself with the pier."

"I believe we are going to feature the new theatre in the next couple of weeks. Can I ask you, Lauren, is this your first stage musical?"

Lauren fluttered her eyelashes as they touched the edge of her turban, looking directly into the camera. "One has done opera of course, La Scala and the Coliseum, don't you know. I have also appeared in a couple of Gilbert and Sullivan productions, the public raved about my Fairy Queen in *Iolanthe* and my *Patience* was something to behold, everyone who was anyone said so at the time. But this will be my first actual stage musical. Of course, Barbra was wonderful in the film, though perhaps a little too young. I will bring a new angle to my Dolly, you can count on it."

"And will you perform eight shows a week?" asked Jane, consulting her notes. "Some find it all too much and rely on an understudy."

Lauren put her hand to her brow and closed her eyes. "An understudy indeed, I am a professional and I will perform eight times a week. My assistant, dear Milly, will ensure I get the proper rest and she has been taking me though my paces where the musical numbers are concerned."

"There is talk that the production may tour following its five-week engagement?"

"I should like nothing more, it would be a shame to change the cast, who I must say are top notch, but I expect there will be a press release about that soon, so I mustn't say too much."

"Will you be following the costumes of the original Broadway production or lean more towards the Streisand film?"

"Neither," said Lauren. "I have discussed this in some detail with the production team and I will not be wearing the red gown for the Harmonia Gardens scene where I make my entrance to the sounds of the title number."

"Can you share with us what colour that particular gown will be?"

"Purple and black my dear," said Lauren, leaning forward in her chair. "I want to put my own mark on it."

"Before we conclude, I understand you have a book coming out about your life in the theatre."

"Yes, that's right Jane. My assistant came up with the title *It's the Voice You Know*; I had intended it to be called *Swathed in Song*. But I went with Milly's suggestion, I have no idea how she thought of the title, but the publishers seemed to like it."

"Well Lauren, thank you for coming in and talking about this exciting moment in theatre history. I would like to wish you every success in *Hello Dolly* which opens of Friday 27 July at 7:30."

"Thank you so much for inviting me. I will make sure that Milly pops a couple of complimentary tickets in the post to you."

"That was the lovely Lauren Du Barrie, now it is back to Graham."

As Lauren made her way off the set she called to Milly who had been waiting in the corridor. "What a thrill, Milly dear, now I must have some lemon and honey, it's the voice you know."

Milly smiled and held up a thermos flask. "Your lemon and honey coming up."

* * *

The Little Playhouse Rehearsals

The rehearsal for "Death in the Scullery" – a thriller in three acts by D. W. Twitt

The action takes place in Claremont House

Lady Sedgewick	Constance Anderson
Lord Sedgewick	Fred Hughes
Sara Harris the maid	Julia Burton
Rubella Jones	Sue Wilson
Clive Clunes	Edmund Green
Mrs Danby, the cook	Edith Harris
Thomas Farmer	Patrick Prowse
Inspector Cross	William Forbes

As the curtain rises, Lady Sedgewick is seen entering into the drawing room slowly followed by her husband, they are both wearing black and Lord Sedgewick heads towards the drinks cabinet as Lady Sedgwick stands centre stage removing her gloves.

Lady S: I am so pleased that is all over. I loved Aunt Poll dearly but why she had to leave us such detail for her funeral service one can only wonder. At least Uncle Cedric had the good fortune to die five years ago leaving her some kind of life on her own.

Who has ever heard of having the hymn, *Fight the Good Fight* at a funeral and quite what that vicar was rambling on about I have no idea. To my knowledge Aunt Poll was never connected to the girl guides *(she pauses playing with the clasp her handbag)*.

Where is that girl when one needs her? Sarah, Sarah come along dear, I haven't got all day.

(Sarah the maid enters stage left in a bit of a fluster)

Sarah: Sorry your ladyship, I was helping Cook with some vegetables, she's a bit behind.

Lord S: Judging by her derriere, she is a lot behind. *(Pours a large whiskey and downs it in one)*

Lady S: That's enough of that, if you don't mind. Sarah please take my coat and bag to my room and lay out my afternoon outfit, the blue with the frilled blouse and a string of pearls should do it. I must look my best when our guests arrive.

(Sarah takes the coat, bag and gloves and heads for the staircase to the right of the stage).

Lady S: Quick sticks my girl, I shall be up there in ten minutes and I don't wish to be kept waiting. Honestly, one really cannot get the staff these days.

Lord S: I say Nancy, that's a bit harsh even for you. Have a snifter, it might help settle your nerves; it has been quite a day.

Lady S: Unlike you dear, I do not find comfort in the bottom of a bottle. Don't forget you need to change.

Lord S: Well there won't be anyone laying my clothes out for me, not since you let old Joe go.

Lady S: The man had one foot in the grave, far too slow, besides you don't really need a servant, you are quite capable of managing on your own.

(Lord S snorts and pours another drink)

Lady S: I think I can feel one of my heads coming along and it would happen today of all days. I should have put off our guests. That's the trouble living in the country, friends expect to pitch up at any time and take advantage of our hospitality.

Ray Darnell clapped his hands. "Can we stop right there please! Fred, you are not making the most of Lord Sedgewick's lines, we ran through this a couple of days ago and Julia darling, you need to give Sarah a bit more energy and you should run up those stairs and be at the top before Fred has finished his lines. Constance, marvellous as ever, I love that business with the handbag it's a nice touch. Right let's take it from the top and can we get these lights adjusted please? There is an awful shadow on the staircase and can someone please top up the decanter?"

The rehearsal continued with Ray stopping and starting the company and going over a scene again and again. Constance, ever the professional, was becoming tired and thought Ray was really over-doing the direction and when he had moved onto a couple of more scenes involving some of the others, she stood up and clapped her hands.

"Ray dear, I do think you are over thinking this a tad. You know as well as I do that once we have done a complete run through of the play, things will naturally fall into place."

Ray, who didn't take kindly to being interrupted, decided to swallow his pride and nodded. "As you so rightly put it Connie darling, perhaps we should all break for some lunch and be back in an hour."

Everyone heaved a sigh of relief and left the theatre with most of them heading to the Toasted Teacake with Ray and William going off for a pub lunch; Ray felt that a pint would settle his nerves.

Alfred was in the pub enjoying a ploughman's and a shandy and beckoned Ray and William to join him.

"Rehearsals going well?" Alfred asked.

William busied himself with his pint and Ray smiled, "Well Alfred you know how these things are, teething problems, but nothing that won't be ironed out before the opening."

"I am pleased to hear it. Maud informs me that the bookings are coming in steadily so you should have a good season."

"I do hope so," Ray replied "if it all goes well I could take these plays to other resorts. *Wardrobe Doors* is still touring since the season ended last year and doing good business despite having a change of cast."

William grinned. "I think my wife had been hit by a flying doorknob once too often to consider touring with it."

"How is the lovely Constance?" enquired Alfred.

"As lovely as ever," said William. "She does enjoy her work, which makes it so much easier for the rest of us. One thing about Constance is that she has always been a professional and never demanded attention, not like some of the actresses I have worked with in the past."

"That is why she is always a delight to direct," said Ray. "She takes it all in her stride and is a great source of help to some of the newer ones who come along, takes them under her wing. I remember directing Lizzie Britain many years ago and she was a complete nightmare, she demanded the best of everything, was forever upstaging the other members of the company and was a pain in the arse, to be brutally frank."

"I had one or two run-ins with her," William said with feeling. "The dear lady has since gone to the great theatre in the sky and I say amen to that."

"The day of her funeral, the chapel was quite empty apart from two others and me," said Ray taking a sup of his pint. "There was one single flower on her coffin and the eulogy, which she no doubt had written herself, went on about how loved she was in the profession."

"Constance refused to go," said William, "and so did many others, they do say you reap what you sow."

A burst of song from the jukebox echoed around the bar, Jim Reeves' *He'll Have to Go* seemed quite apt and the three men continued their lunch in silence.

Rehearsals at The Little Playhouse had begun on Monday 25th June to give the company a whole week before their opening. They were to rehearse at the theatre every morning and early afternoon with the variety artistes for the evening offering, rehearsing late afternoon into the evening. Most cast members were familiar with the theatre and the Brokencliff area and had secured the lodgings they had the previous year. The variety artistes who were less familiar were scattered across the area with some taking rooms in Gorleston and Lowestoft.

Bookings were quite healthy and Maud and Barbara were kept quite busy at the box office. Alfred looked in on the proceedings and saw that everything was coming together. When he watched a run-through of the variety show, he wondered whether Donna Quinn might be interested in doing something similar the following year and kept her in mind; he would ask her when he next met with her.

Alfred thought that he really should try and get something in the theatre during the weeks of June and would put that in action the following year. The circus opened in Great Yarmouth in late May and the summer shows began to open in June including *The Old Tyme Music Hall* in Gorleston while his theatre remained dark. With Joe's park and his hotel doing good business the theatre was missing out. Even if he couldn't get the repertory in, he could at least get together a small variety show for the evening. He made a mental note to raise it with Rita's Angels.

Edwin had been getting to grips with his job at the Golden Sands and was enjoying each day which seemed to bring a new challenge. Some of the backstage boys had previously worked at the theatre and were more than happy to help Edwin settle in. Getting the hang of the lighting gantry and the sound system were something Edwin found intriguing and his eagerness to learn impressed those around him. It soon became apparent that he wasn't afraid of hard work and helped his colleagues in the same manner the late Jim Donnell had done. He had made a list of things that needed doing each day and ticked them off as he went along. The backstage boys were briefed each morning about what to expect and everything ran quite smoothly. Any small hiccups were soon ironed out. The arrival of the scenery for *Hello Dolly* would be a challenge. They had been hired from London and were the ones used in the production starring Mary Martin and later Dora Bryan. The new fly tower would be able to hold much more than had previously been possible. The turntable on the stage would enable a scene to be set while another was playing. A huge trailer carrying a life-size steam engine and carriages would be the greatest challenge and would be run on small electric rails in the stage floor. This would transport Dolly and her friends across the stage and would be a spectacular sight to behold. The train had been specially designed by a local company and had not formed part of the original London production. It was June's hope that it would bring a wow factor to the show. Edwin knew from meetings with the production company that this show would make or break the opening of the theatre and he had every confidence it would do so.

Mona had watched Edwin work and on a rare occasion she bumped into Rita in the market place and expressed her observations about the new stage manager. Rita glad to hear of the news gave Mona her thanks and knew the production was in good hands.

Chapter Seven – July

THE LITTLE PLAYHOUSE – Brokencliff-on-Sea

Rita Ricer in association with Ray Darnell and
Alfred Barton
presents

For the Summer Season from
Monday 2 July until Saturday 1 September 1973

Afternoons at 2pm (except Sun) –

Up the Garden Path – a farce in 3 acts by Francis
Brainbridge
Death in the Scullery – a thriller in 3 acts by D W Twitt
featuring the Clifftop Players under the direction of Ray
Darnell

Week 1 – **Mon – Wed** "Up the Garden Path" / **Thurs – Sat**
"Death in the Scullery"
Week 2 – **Mon – Wed** "Death in the Scullery" / **Thurs – Sat**
– "Up the Garden Path"
then alternating weeks – see two plays in one week!

Bookable in advance from the box office
60p and 50p
**Special Offer – Monday and Thursday Matinees all
seats 45p**

****

Nightly at 7.45 (except Sun)
"Stargaze Showtime"
Starring
"Dean and Layla Dubrette"
"Only a Rose –I Love You"
with
"Comedian" **Jack Newbury**
"Magic Fingers" **Tom and Tilly Mystery**
Miss Penny's Puppets
The Clifftop Gaiety Girls
Providing the music
Phil Yovell and Darren Yates

Bookable in advance from the Box Office
75p and 65p
Special offer – Monday evenings only all seats 60p
The programme

"Up the Garden Path" A farce in three acts by Francis
Brainbridge

The setting is "Gables Guest House"

Betty Gable – the landlady	Edith Harris
Edward Gable – her husband	Fred Hughes

The guests

Corrine Barton	Constance Anderson
George Trent	William Forbes
Molly Mangle	Sue Wilson
Morton Green	Edmund Green
Cary Simon	Julia Burton
Freddie Boon	Patrick Prowse

"Death in the Scullery" – a thriller in three acts by D W Twitt

The action takes place in "Claremont House"

Lady Sedgewick	Constance Anderson
Lord Sedgewick	Fred Hughes
Sara Harris the maid	Julia Burton
Rubella Jones	Sue Wilson
Clive Clunes	Edmund Green
Mrs Danby, the cook	Edith Harris
Thomas Farmer	Patrick Prowse
Inspector Cross	William Forbes

The programme

"STARGAZE SHOWTIME"

- ❖ **Opus One** – Phil Yovell at the Baby Grand and Darren Yates (percussion)
- ❖ **"Come to the Party"** – The Clifftop Gaiety Girls
- ❖ **"Have you Heard the One?"** – Jack Newbury
- ❖ **"On Moonlight Bay"** – The Clifftop Gaiety Girls
- ❖ **"Strings and Things"** – Miss Penny's Puppets
- ❖ **"Make Mine Magic"** – Tom and Tilly Mystery

Interval

- ❖ **Opus Two** – Phil Yovell and Darren Yates
- ❖ **"And There's This One Too"** – Jack Newbury
- ❖ **"Music, Music, Music"** – The Clifftop Gaiety Girls

Introduce
The Stars of the Show
DEAN AND LAYLA DUBRETTE

- ❖ The Company say "Goodnight"

THE GOLDEN SANDS THEATRE Gt Yarmouth

June Ashby and Roo Productions
proudly present
Jerry Herman's
"HELLO DOLLY"

Starring Lauren Du Barrie as Dolly Gallagher Levi
and Jacob Manfred as Horace Vandergelder

Opening Friday 27 July 1973 at 7.30
(Thereafter Monday to Saturday at 7.30 and
Matinees Wednesday and Saturday at 2.30)
Strictly Limited Season – must close Saturday 1 Sept
1973

STALLS - £3.50 - £2.50 and £1.00
DRESS CIRCLE - £3.50 and £2.50
Bookable in advance at the Theatre Box Office

***

HELLO DOLLY – Cast in order of appearance

Mrs Dolly Gallagher Levi	Lauren Du Barrie
Ernestina	Sara Maddock
Ambrose Kemper	David Bronx
Horace Vandergelder	Jacob Manfred
Ermengarde	Doreen Rogers
Cornelius Hackl	Thom Harding
Barnaby Tucker	Samuel Matthews
Irene Molloy	Gaye Tilling
Minnie Fay	Debra Watling
Court Clerk	Cedric Narberth
Mrs Rose	Gladys Kent
Rudolph	Brian Delaney
Judge	Gordon Johns

The studio at Earl's Court was a buzz of excitement as the main cast were meeting for the first time. Last to arrive in a swathe of furs and jewellery, with her assistant Milly trailing behind, was Lauren Du Barrie.

Ray Darnell greeted her with his arms open. "Welcome, dear lady!"

Lauren smiled regally and dropped her furs to the floor with Milly quickly retrieving them. "I am so sorry we are running late, it's the traffic don't you know, one could barely get the Rolls along the Earl's Court Road, so many buses and taxis clogging things up."

"Allow me to introduce you to the cast," said Ray as a bead of sweat ran down his brow; for some reason he had been dreading working with Lauren and was hoping that his doubts would be unfounded. Before Ray could make the first introduction, Jacob Manfred rushed forward and grabbed Lauren by the shoulders.

"Darling Lauren, how wonderful to see you after all these years," he gushed.

Lauren blushed and gazed into his eyes. "Jacob, can you hear my heart pounding? I thought I had read the cast list wrong when I saw your name. To think we are going to be working together again fills me with such delight."

The two looked at each other for some time and the other cast members looked at each other. Ray looked at the floor feeling totally relieved. He had been worried that the two stars would clash.

Lauren took Jacob's hand and they both turned to face the others.

"Forgive us," said Lauren. "So rude of us to interrupt dear Ray's introductions. I should explain that Jacob and I toured Australia in Rose Marie and again in Canada. We became firm friends and now fate, as fate would have it, has bought us back together and I couldn't be happier."

"I second that," said Jacob beaming a dazzling white smile. "But now we must hand the floor over to our director Mr Ray Darnell. Ray, as you were."

Ray, recovering from this unexpected turn of good fortune, felt himself relax and one by one introduced each member of the cast giving a little bit of their theatrical background for good measure.

"Today we will generally be getting to know each other, running through a few scenes from this wonderful musical and then as the week progresses we will be joined by our ace choreographer Jane Kenton."

"It's James Kenton," Doreen Rogers piped up.

Ray, who had deliberately said Jane, smiled. "Sorry company, how silly of me, I meant to say James of course."

"I bet he didn't," Doreen whispered to Samuel Matthews who was standing beside her. "There is some history there, let's grab some tea later and I will spill."

Samuel, who wasn't the least interested in gossip, nodded politely and thanked his lucky stars that Doreen was not playing his love interest.

Suddenly the door of the studio burst open and in ran James Kenton, tossing his long mane of blonde hair and dazzling the room with a broad and white toothy smile. His tight jeans left nothing to the imagination and his floaty shirt was unbuttoned to reveal his hairy chest. His shoes were high-heeled and his fingers were adorned in more jewellery than a show girl.

"Hi babes, sorry to drop in unannounced as it were but I just wanted to wish you all the best of luck and to say how much I am looking forward to working with you all."

Ray looked James up and down. "James what a lovely surprise, I see you are wearing your Mary Janes, are you working with the dancers today."

"Ray babes," said James, air-kissing the sides of Ray's cheeks. "You know me darling, I never stop. I won't interrupt your workshop further. We must do lunch sometime, chow for now." And with that, James exited with a toss of his hair and a hand waving in the air.

"Speak of the devil," said Ray, and turned back to the cast. "That was our choreographer James and we will be seeing more of her, sorry him, later in the week. Now I think we are all in need of a cup of coffee and then we can get things rolling."

As if on cue, crashing through the door, a lady pushing a tea trolley entered which she deposited in the corner of studio. "Tea's up. Help yourselves to milk and sugar. I've put out some chocolate digestives and custard creams. If you need anything else, give me a shout. My name is Florrie and you'll find me in the kitchen area, second right down the corridor. I've got another group in later so I best get slicing my baps." And with that Florrie exited.

"Milly darling, lemon and honey for me, it's the voice you know."

And so began the first day of rehearsals for *Hello Dolly*.

* * *

"So, any news?" asked Muriel Evans accepting a cup of tea from her neighbour Freda Boggis.

Freda gave Muriel one her knowing expressions, "Mrs Sutton's daughter has given birth to a baby girl."

"Mother and baby well?"

"They are now," said Freda taking a bite of a digestive. "She had a beach birth."

Muriel smiled, "Surely you mean a breech birth, Freda?"

"No, she gave birth on the sand dunes. She was walking along with her mother and suddenly her waters broke. According to Mrs Sutton, it was all hands to the pump. Fortunately, a man was walking his dog and went off to a telephone box to call for an ambulance. Anyway, by the time they arrived, Mrs Sutton was holding her granddaughter's head in one hand and holding onto her daughter's hand with the other."

"It must have been very frightening," said Muriel, with a concerned expression.

"Not for Mrs Sutton, remember her folks ran a travelling ghost train for years. I don't think fear came into it. Mind you, she can be like a bull in a Chinese shop at times."

There was a pause while Muriel tried to get her head around the last part of Freda's report.

"Have they named the baby girl?" asked Muriel, coming to.

"Oh yes," Freda replied. "They have called her Sandie."

"How apt," Muriel replied.

"Poor old Mrs Drake passed away three days ago. Lovely old gal she was, mind you she was a good age, 93, but she was a bright as a button even towards the end. Popped off in the middle of *Crossroads* and she had only dipped her nets that afternoon. Of course, you heard about Jessie's daughter who took up with that fella from Lowestoft, they say he is a philanderer."

"I hope you put Jessie right Freda, you do know what a philanderer is?"

Freda nodded. "Of course I do, I said to her you tell your Suzie from me, there can be nothing more boring than going out with a man who collects stamps as a hobby."

Muriel made a mental note to give Jessie a call and took another sip of her tea. "Is there any other news?"

"No, I think that's all at the moment" said Freda scratching her bosom. She was wearing a new bra and it was giving her gip. "Have another cup of tea, Muriel?"

Muriel accepted the tea and then, mulling over something she had heard, decided to share it with her friend. "By the way Freda, I have heard that Lilly's cottage in Brokencliff is up for sale; wherever she has gone she isn't planning on coming back."

"Well I'll be bunkered," said Freda with a gasp. "All of those terrible incidents with the gardener and the mushrooms would have died down in time. People do gossip unnecessarily about these things."

Muriel nodded. "Yes, they do, don't they?"

There was silence for a few minutes while both ladies gathered their thoughts on what had been said.

"Oh, I forgot to tell you," said Freda banging down her cup and saucer, causing some tea to spill on her newly laundered tablecloth. "Freddie's fish-and-chip has had to close."

Muriel looked astounded. "But he always does such a good business there. The locals rave about his battered sausage."

"Oh, he's not closing permanently," said Freda. "Apparently the ceiling fell out of his back passage."

Muriel choked on her last mouthful of tea.

Freda drained the last drops from the teapot into her cup. "It'll be a few weeks before he's up and running again."

Muriel nodded. "Yes, by the sounds it, I think it will."

Monday 23 July

The Golden Sands theatre had been a hive of activity and the sets for *Hello Dolly* were now in place. The costumes and wigs were delivered and sorted and a buzz of excitement was felt throughout the building. The cast had arrived the day before. The only person who was not yet present was Lauren Du Barrie. As everyone assembled on the stage to be given further direction from Ray Darnell, the rear doors of the auditorium opened and one fur-clad Lauren Du Barrie made her entrance, with Milly shuffling behind with bags dangling from her arms.

"Good morning everyone, I am so sorry to be a trifle late but one had problems with the Rolls, don't you know," she exclaimed, her voice filling the theatre.

Ray turned on his heels. "And what were they my dear, cheese or ham?"

The cast tittered at this. Lauren proceeded down the aisle like a galleon in full sail. "My dear Ray, how you love to jest. I've been very busy, my darling, settling into a quaint little cottage over at Hemsby. Milly dear, do hurry up and get to the dressing room there's a love, lemon and honey. It's the voice you know."

As Lauren discarded her furs in row F of the stalls, she approached the side steps of the stage, her heels nearly missing the treads, causing her to wobble, but she overcame this and with a radiant smile stood centre-stage, awaiting further instruction.

Ray retreated to the front of the auditorium and addressed the cast. "Now that we are all here, I thought it would be a good idea for you all to walk through the show, paying special attention to the coloured markers on the stage for each scene. This afternoon we will go through all the production numbers when the full orchestra will be with us."

"Why aren't they here now?" asked Jacob, who was playing Horace.

"They are stuck on the Acle Straight in a broken-down coach, but I have been assured they will be here this afternoon. The landlord of a local pub has kept me informed and has been providing refreshments to the boys."

Jacob coughed. "I do hope they won't turn up inebriated."

The cast laughed at the suggestion.

"They have been given coffee and sandwiches as far as I am aware," said Ray, wishing he had never mentioned the incident. "Now, let's get down to business."

"I must change my shoes," said Lauren, rushing to the wings. "I simply must be comfortable if we are going to be on our feet the best part of the morning."

Jamie Dormy, the general manager of the theatre with Edwin Dawson, the stage manager, watched this scene unfold from the dress circle.

"You are going to need to be on your toes with this lot," said Jamie with a smile. "Think you can handle it?"

Edwin nodded. "Oh, don't worry Mr Dormy, I will soon have them eating out of my hand."

Jamie laughed. "Good, I'm pleased to hear it. And you must call me Jamie, we don't stand on ceremony here, though I should imagine that some of the cast will need to be addressed accordingly, especially Miss Du Barrie."

"I best get on," said Edwin, turning to leave. "Mrs Buckle wants a word and it doesn't bode well to keep her waiting."

"Arh yes, the great Mona Buckle. She is someone else to look out for, though a good worker if all I have heard is correct."

"I mustn't forget she likes her tea at eleven and is partial to a bourbon or custard cream."

Jamie laughed again and followed Edwin down the staircase of the circle, where the sounds of a clanging bucket and mop could be heard coming from the theatre reception area.

Mona looked up from her work. "Good morning Mr Dormy and Mr Dawson, it's a fine morning for it."

The men both nodded. "When you are ready for your chat Mrs Buckle," said Edwin, "I will be in the office."

"I am ready now Mr Dawson," said Mona, propping her bucket and mop against the wall. "I need to talk to you about the supplies and the contract cleaners."

Jamie watched as the two went by and smiled to himself, grateful that he wouldn't be dealing with Mona on a one-to-one basis now that a new agreement had been reached.

Cheryl Wong, his secretary, handed him some post and letters that needed his signature. "Mr Dormy, Selina in box office would like a word when you have a moment."

Jamie laid the mail and letters down on his desk and went straight to the box office. Selina smiled as he approached.

"Oh, thank you for coming along so quickly," she said, opening the door and allowing Jamie in. "We have a problem on the opening night, I received this, it should have come to you really but someone must have given my name out. You know we are fully booked, where are we going to sit this lady and her husband?"

Jamie read the letter and whistled. "Best keep this under wraps, as the letter states, no advance publicity of their arrival and it wouldn't be good if the cast got to hear about this. Have we got any house seats on hold?"

"Well there are only four centre front stalls being held for Lauren Du Barrie."

"Then reserve two of those please Selina and I will inform Miss Du Barrie that owing to an error on my part, she has only two house seats."

"She won't be happy," said Selina, imaging the woman she had just seen sweep into the theatre. "She seems terribly grand."

"She a theatrical," said Jamie. "She always behaves that way and, Selina, do address me as Jamie, we are all work colleagues here."

Selina blushed. "Yes Mr Dormy, I mean Jamie, I will, thank you."

* * *

"So you see, Mr Dawson, those contract cleaners are not doing their work properly, hence the reason I was cleaning the reception area this morning."

"And are they doing the auditorium properly?" asked Edwin

Looking around her, Mona huffed and her eye began to water, always a bad sign. "Well, they seem to have cleaned after a fashion, but not to the Mona Buckle standard, you understand. The brass rails at the back of the stalls need careful attention. I will have to become firmer with them."

"Would you like me to have a word with them?"

"A manager of your standing shouldn't have to get involved. I just wanted, if you would be so kind, a little guidance about how to go about it."

Edwin smiled. "Well, Mrs Buckle, the gentle touch would be the first approach. Point out to them the areas that need their attention and give them a couple of days to get it under their belts. If they don't improve, then a firmer hand will be needed, a warning of such. If that fails, we can put them under notice for not fulfilling their contract and engage our own cleaning staff. It is of the upmost importance that we keep the theatre pristine at all costs. If what I have heard is true, the theatre will be running almost 52 weeks of the year and we must ensure consistency across the board."

This was quite a speech coming from Edwin, but he had learnt some lessons from Jamie on how to handle certain situations.

Mona nodded and seemed happy with his advice. "Thank you, Mr Dawson, I won't trouble you further." Mona heaved herself to her feet.

"Mrs Buckle I wonder if you would join me at eleven for a cup of tea and a biscuit, I like to take a break at that time."

Mona beamed. "That would be most acceptable, Mr Dawson. Eleven is an ideal time for refreshment and reflection."

Edwin watched her leave the office; she certainly was a character and the strains of *The Old Rugged Cross* could be heard, which made Jamie smile.

* * *

That afternoon with the orchestra in the pit, the numbers of the musical began. Lauren was on top form and her attack on the opening number, *I Put My Hand in Here* was both melodic and funny. She paused at the right moments and even some of the chorus had a hard time suppressing their giggles.

When they reached the half-way mark to the number, *Before the Parade Passes By*, Ray had a further announcement to make.

"I've decided that we need to pad this number out; we have a strong chorus of dancers and singers here, but I thought we could go further. I have invited local amateur dramatic groups in the area to provide extras, which will come down the aisles of the auditorium with banners and flags to make the whole scene fuller and livelier."

"But won't that make the choreography difficult?" said Lauren, stepping out of character to address Ray.

The choreographer, James Kenton who had been sitting in the back row of the stalls came forward. "No, Miss Du Barrie, it won't be a problem at all. There will be at least 60 extras per performance and they have been kitted out in the appropriate costumes. The aim is that they arrive ten minutes before the scene starts and will enter from the rear of the auditorium with about ten of them doing likewise in the dress circle. I have been in the town for a couple of weeks meeting with the two societies

I have, sorry Ray, and I have approached and have rehearsed them to within an inch of their lives."

At that moment a group of 60 banner-flag waving amateurs entered the theatre and marched down the aisles.

The cast applauded. "It is a wonderful idea," said Lauren. "I just hope we won't have any problems with Equity. I take it we are not paying these good people?"

Ray broke in. "We have agreed to make a donation to each of the societies as a 'thank you' and, besides, it gives these thespians a crack at a professional production."

Everyone smiled. "Now let's take it from the top," said James Kenton. "Extras, take up your places and let us do justice to this ingenious idea of Ray's."

Ray almost blushed. It was the first time that James had complimented him on anything.

The orchestra struck up and Lauren began the number with her usual aplomb. As the parade began to build, the extras made their entrance and the auditorium became a blaze of music and colour.

Mona had come into the theatre to check on the brass railings and stood and watched in wonder, taken aback by the spectacle of the whole thing.

Edwin had been backstage ensuring that his boys were ready with scene changes and props. He understood a lot was riding on the musical and he didn't want his section to mess up. Most of the backstage staff had worked in the theatre in the days of Jim Donnell, but they never compared the management skills and capability of Edwin with Jim. Edwin was an easy-going young man and he made them all feel valued and that in turn earned him their respect.

Friday 27 July

"Milly, I don't think I have felt so nervous since that theatre cat in Edinburgh gave birth on my fur stole."

Milly handed Lauren some honey and lemon. "I don't know why you are getting so worked up, the dress rehearsal was spot on this afternoon. The box office has notices saying 'house full'. The whole cast are simply a delight to be around and so friendly, you are very lucky to be playing such a prestigious role."

Lauren wiped a tear from her eye. "Yes, Milly dear you are right."

There was a knock on the door. "Flowers for Miss Du Barrie," said Edwin, coming in with the largest bouquet he had ever seen.

"For me?" exclaimed Lauren. "There must be some mistake, who would send little old me, flowers on opening night."

Milly went in search of a vase. "Who would dare not to send her flowers on opening night?" she muttered under her breath.

"Oh, darling how wonderful! Rita has sent a 'good luck' message with these gorgeous flowers."

Milly returned with a vase followed by Jacob, who was holding out a small posy of flowers and a box of chocolates. "For my leading lady, break a leg my dear. I am sure we are going to have a wonderful run together."

Lauren kissed Jacob on the cheek. "You are an angel, thank you so much," and then, quite unlike Lauren, she held out a gift-wrapped box to Jacob "A little something for you, Jacob as a token of my appreciation for being a wonderful Horace."

Jacob tore open the paper and opened the gold box. It was a pair of gold cufflinks.

"My dear lady, how very kind of you, I shall treasure them," he exclaimed and returned the kiss on the cheek.

"This is your fifteen-minute call," the announcement over the tannoy echoed through the dressing rooms.

Jacob bowed and left the dressing room as Milly helped Lauren with the wig.

"I am so pleased we settled on blonde, that red wig was awful," said Milly. "Some people look good with red hair. You are not one of them."

Lauren was going to reply but decided to leave well alone, it was unlike Milly to be so sharp.

The five-minute call was sounded and Lauren made her way to the side of the stage, Milly stood ready with lemon and honey should it be needed.

The auditorium had filled up. Rita, Jenny and Elsie were sitting fifth row centre in the stalls, several local dignitaries were scattered about the theatre and Lady Samantha and Sir Harold were in the front row of the dress circle. Mona Buckle, along with some of the other staff had secured seats at the back of the stalls.

The conductor appeared in the orchestra pit and, as a spotlight lit him, raised his baton and the overture of *Hello Dolly* began as theatre lights dimmed.

The curtain rose and the audience applauded, then on cue Lauren Du Barrie dressed in a blue and white frock with a bustle and a stunning blue hat entered to the refrains of the chorus singing "Call on Dolly, if your eldest daughter needs a friend…".

The scene with the steam engine received gasps from the audience and Edwin who was watching from the wings heaved a sigh of relief, everything had worked and gone according to plan.

The final scene of act one was another highlight, the extras entered during the rendition of *Before the Parade Passes By* and, with their colourful banners and costumes, the auditorium became part of the scene that was happening on stage.

The audience applauded and cheered as the curtain came down. They filed out to the bar or to the usherettes selling ice cream. Everyone was talking about how wonderful the show was.

June Ashby met Rita at the back of theatre. "Well Rita, do you think we have pulled it off?"

Rita nodded. "I did have my doubts, especially about Lauren, but I have to say, fair play to them all, they have the audience in the palm of their hands."

June handed Rita a gin and tonic.

"Did I spot a certain actress in the audience?"

June nodded. "Not a word, it is meant to be a surprise, I just hope the gentlemen of the press haven't spotted her."

Jenny had gone back stage to speak to Lauren. "My dear, you are quite marvellous, you have obviously nailed this part, I can't wait until the second half, and there is the big Dolly number to look forward to."

Lauren thanked Jenny. "I must say, I couldn't have done this without good old Milly, that girl knows every line, every song and has been at my side since the day I accepted the role. I am very lucky to have her with me."

Milly who had busied herself at the back of the dressing room heard the comment and smiled, it was nice to be appreciated and it didn't happen often, not to the Millicent Lansburys of this world, anyway.

The curtain rose on the second half of the show and then half way through came the moment everyone had been waiting for, the Harmonia Gardens scene. Twenty dancing waiters, lead by head waiter Rudolph, sang the opening refrain of *Hello Dolly* as a very glamorous Lauren descended the wide staircase in a stunning purple and black gown with matching feathers in her hair. There were gasps from the audience as the routine got in full swing. Calls for more at the end of the number resulted in a short reprise from Lauren and her boys, as she called them, and the show continued to its conclusion.

The audience cheered and whoops of "well done" and "bravo" filled the air. Lauren was visibly moved and took eight curtain calls. Milly escorted her back to her dressing room and gave her a big hug.

Lauren was quite emotional. "I really couldn't have done this without you Milly. I know I don't very often praise or thank you, but you really are a very faithful and loyal companion, bless you."

A knock on the door was followed by June Ashby entering. "Lauren, my dear I must congratulation you on a wonderful performance. There is someone here who would very much like to meet you." June stood aside. "Lauren, I would like you meet Dora Bryan."

Lauren gasped in surprise and stood up to shake the hand of Miss Bryan. "I can't tell you what an honour it is to meet you."

June motioned for Milly to leave the room. "I think we will leave you two ladies to chat," she said diplomatically.

The party that followed afterwards was a great success although Dora Bryan did not stay as she had to return to London. Lauren could not believe that the star of stage and screen had come to see her in the role that she has taken over from Mary Martin at Drury Lane back in the sixties. Everyone was congratulating everyone else and even Mona was heard to say that she had not enjoyed herself so much in years, a compliment indeed, coming from Mrs Buckle.

The reviews that appeared in the local press the following day were singing the praises of the company and stated how brave it had been to launch the new theatre with a musical rather than a traditional summer show. Lauren read the reviews as she ate her light breakfast of boiled eggs and toast. Milly hummed happily and was pleased that it has all turned out so well, but things were to take a turn, that no one had anticipated.

Saturday 28 July

Madge Brinton got into second gear. "Not long now, Mum."

Her mother Annie Lucas, who was chewing a sweet, looked at her daughter. "I don't know why we have to go to Brokencliff-on-Sea again, we went there last year."

Madge sighed, it was always the same. Her mother was never satisfied. "When I asked where you would like to go what did you say to me?"

Annie chewed her sweet. "I can't remember."

"Your very words were, if your father is going off to Blackpool again we could go to that place we went to last year. You said how much you wanted to visit Norwich Castle. So that is where we are going."

"What? The castle?"

"No Mum, Brokencliff. We are staying at that nice hotel, The Beach Croft, you liked it there. We can have a day out to Norwich Castle and take in the sights. The receptionist at the hotel has reserved tickets for us to see *Hello Dolly* starring Lauren Du Barrie at the Golden Sands theatre in Great Yarmouth."

"Is she that woman we saw last year at that little theatre?"

"That's right Mum, Lauren Du Barrie."

"I don't like her," replied Annie. "I'd rather go to the circus."

"But Mum, it won't be like it was last year. Lauren is playing Dolly Levi, it's a musical. You remember, Barbra Streisand did the film version."

"She's not in it is she?"

"No, she isn't."

"Thank the Lord for small mercies, I never rated her."

"Oh Mum, do cheer up, the weather looks promising and I am sure once we are settled in at the hotel, we will have a lovely time."

"I'll be the judge of that," said Annie.

They arrived at their destination and a parking space had been reserved for them in the hotel's car park.

Madge approached the reception desk and was greeted with a smile. "Welcome back ladies," said the young man behind the desk. "You have the same rooms as you had last year."

"Oh, that's nice, isn't it Mum, the same rooms."

"I hope they've hoovered."

"Mum behave, of course they have," replied Madge, taking the keys from the young man. "Sorry about that."

The young man winked at Madge. "I will have a porter bring up your suitcases and a tray of tea. I expect you've had a long journey."

Annie's face lit up. "That would be very nice, young man, and if you've got any biscuits going spare, they would be most welcome."

"Leave it with me, madam."

"Here we are," said Madge, opening her mother's bedroom door.

"It's a different bedspread and they've changed the wallpaper."

"Well I expect they refurbish every year," said Madge. "I'll just go into my room and I'll come back for the tea."

Annie walked round the room and ran her finger across the surfaces. There was not a speck of dust. She then got down on her hands and knees and looked under the bed just as room service arrived with the tea tray.

"Are you alright, madam?" said the young boy by the name of Pete. "Can I help you?"

Annie blushed. "I thought I had dropped something," she said, getting up.

* * *

Joe Dean was kept busy welcoming families to Finnegan's Wake. Some had stayed before but he was pleased that new guests were ready to take a chance on the newly refurbished park.

"I say Duggie, look at all this space," said Mrs Grey as she looked around the place that was to be their home for the next two weeks. "The kids will love this, get them out of the car, they will need some orange juice."

A couple who were also new to this holiday experience were much impressed with their static home on wheels and told Joe they would recommend it to their friends. It was cheaper than staying at a hotel and you weren't confined to meal times like you were in guest houses. The Toasted Teacake across the road had seen increased business since the new park had opened and The Fisherman's was a hive of activity in the evenings.

Joe always directed his guests to the offerings at Owlerton Hall and The Little Playhouse and both had seen an upturn in patrons. Alfred was particularly pleased to be able to post 'House Full' notices at several performances and Maud and Barbara were kept busy, trying to get people to return on a different date when things weren't so busy.

The local buses were ferrying people between Brokencliff and Great Yarmouth, meaning that the holidaymakers' money was being spread across the resorts.

Joe's bookings were looking healthy until the end of September and he was beginning to see his investment working to his advantage.

"Well, you are certainly on the right track, Joe," said Phil, as she put together his order, and this little shop has never been so busy."

"I am really pleased," said Joe. "The regulars I've had at the park seem very pleased with the changes and the new ones are bowled over by what is on offer. Putting local literature in the homes has definitely got people visiting the theatre and Owlerton Hall and of course they all require provisions, and what better place to get them than here in Tidy Stores?"

"I have noticed that Lady Samantha from the Hall seems to be out and about a bit more than is usual. Normally you glimpse her as she sails through in her chauffeur-driven car."

"I think she has finally come around to embracing the community in which she lives," said Joe. "She needs the business as much as the rest of us. Personally, I find her to be quite charming."

"You usually find that with the gentry," said Phil, putting a packet of cereal in Joe's order that she had forgotten. "I am going to pop up there one afternoon when things are quiet and have a look around for myself."

"Well you could always ask Charles to mind the shop for you, I am sure he wouldn't mind for an hour or two."

"Do you think Charles could manage this?"

"He'd be okay once he got started," said Joe with a grin. "Besides it would give him a break from his hospital visits."

"I will keep that in mind," said Phil, acknowledging some customers who had just wandered in.

"Let me take that order and get out of your way," said Joe. "You are in for another busy day." He bent down to give Dingle a stroke and the little dog barked in delight.

"Thanks Joe," said Phil waving him off. "Now madam, how can I help you?"

* * *

Sunday 29 July

At breakfast Madge suggested to her mother that they take in a tour of Owlerton Hall. "It says here they have a falconry display and you can see the birds of prey close up."

"Didn't we go there last time?" asked Annie, buttering some more toast.

"Yes, we did, but it's been done up a bit since then and, according to this, the gardens have been redesigned."

"Well they certainly needed it," Annie replied with feeling. "If we go there this morning, can we go into Great Yarmouth this afternoon? I want to get some little gifts to take back home."

"We can do," said Madge pleased that her mother was actually asking to do something instead of complaining. "We could also book some tickets for the circus for later during the week."

"Why do we want to do that?"

"Because you said you wanted to go to the circus."

Sometimes, thought Madge, it was like dealing with a child.

Monday 30 July

The cast from The Little Playhouse had been along to see *Hello Dolly* and they all agreed that Lauren had nailed the part.

Following a meal in Regent Road later, a few of them carried on their conversation in Divers' Bar in the town.

"She was quite wonderful," said Constance. "I admit I had my doubts, but she was very good."

"I thought Debra Watling was very good as Minnie," added Sue Wilson. "I remember seeing her in something a few years ago, a talented young actress."

Edith Harris, who was used to playing second leads in plays, added, "I always wanted to do a musical but never quite had the nerve to audition for any."

"What musicals had you in mind?" asked Fred Hughes, who had dabbled in musicals until he realised he wasn't any good at them.

"Something like *South Pacific*," said Edith.

Fred laughed. "I could just see you in a grass skirt."

"I think you have been exceptionally talented to be in a musical," said Sue Wilson, who had been nursing a gin and tonic. "You must be able to sing and dance, and act well of course. The last musical I saw was a revival of *The Flower Drum Song*."

"That never really took off the first time around," said Constance, "which was a shame because it has some lovely tunes in, though not on the same level as *The King and I*."

"Thinking of that," said her husband William Forbes, "I often wonder why they cast Gertrude Lawrence in the role of Anna on Broadway."

"Well that's simple, darling," said Constance. "They wanted an English actress to play opposite Yul, and Gertie was as English as they came. It was her that came up with the idea of turning the story into a musical after she had read the book. Besides Gertie had worked a lot with Noel Coward and could sing; well, after a fashion. I understand that the songs were written in a key that Gertie could manage, giving the more difficult numbers to other members of the cast. Poor Gertie died during the run of that show and never knew what a great success it was to become."

"Yes, that was sad," agreed Edith. "It's a shame Yul never came to London to play the role, wasn't it Herbert Lom who played in the original London production?"

"That's right and Valerie Hobson was Anna," said Constance. "Now, is someone going to get another round of drinks in? That barman looks perfectly bored."

"How are we all getting back to our digs?" asked Edith. "I am thinking of taking the bus."

"Let's all take the bus," said Constance, "but we mustn't be too late, you know we have a rehearsal tomorrow, though why we need one at this late stage is beyond me, you'd have thought Ray had enough to do with Dolly."

"You know what he's like, thinks he has spotted something out of the ordinary and just has to be seen to be putting it right," said William.

"Last year I was attacked by bloody knobs from wardrobes and he never put that right."

"But darling you have to admit it was rather funny and the audience loved it."

Constance frowned. "Well I didn't."

That seemed to bring the conversation to a close until fresh drinks had been procured.

Tuesday 31 July

Madge had driven the car over to Norwich and took her mother around the Castle. There were rooms of stuffed animals and historical artefacts and art to look at. Annie was not impressed.

"Why on earth would you want to stuff an animal and put it in a glass case?"

"So people who have never seen a particular animal before can see one."

"You can see animals at the zoo."

"Yes, but not ones that are extinct, that's a dodo you are looking at.

"A what what?"

"A dodo. Come on Mum, let's find the café and have a coffee, I need to take the weight off my feet."

"I told you not to wear them shoes, they pinch your feet. You should have worn some sensible shoes."

"Yes Mum."

* * *

"Just a few things to go over," said Ray, looking at the cast who had assembled on the stage at Brokencliff. "I note that in both plays one or two of you are not hitting the mark, it needs to be tightened up. I have had some notes typed for you all and I would like you all to pay attention to the areas that need addressing." Ray began handing out the papers.

"Well my dear," said Constance. "Wouldn't it be better for us all to discuss this openly? After all, we are among friends."

Ray coughed. His mind was all over the place with the added worry of *Hello Dolly* which seemed to be in his thoughts constantly as if he was waiting for something to go wrong. "Some of it may seem rather trivial, but I don't want us to let things slip."

"So, the fact of the matter is that we may challenge some of your observations and you would rather we didn't do it here and now," said Constance who was quite irritated by the whole idea. "I shall read your comments Ray and will return this paper to you when I have done so. Expect there to be a lot of red ink; I think you get my drift."

Ray blushed. "You can, of course, all stay and go through the notes."

"Well, we could if you had called this meeting for nine instead of twelve, and I am not about to forfeit lunch," said Constance, picking up her handbag. "I'm off to the Toasted Teacake if anyone else would care to join me."

"Well..." said Ray.

"The invitation is not extended to you, Ray," added Constance. Everyone remained silent, it was unlike Constance to be so rude. Everyone nodded at Ray and followed Constance out of the stage door.

"I think you have ruffled a few feathers there," said Alfred, who had been observing from the back of the auditorium.

"Yes, I think you're right. I didn't mean to, but I felt it wrong to just chat to the three responsible."

"Come on old chap, come and have a ploughman's with me in the Fishermen's."

"Thanks Alfred, I think I will."

Wednesday 1 August

"I have to say I do find matinées a chore," said Lauren, accepting the lemon and honey prepared by Milly. "It's the thought of having to do it all again in the evening."

"It is no different to playing twice nightly," said Milly. "At least you get a break between shows on matinée days. The variety artistes are lucky to get 25 minutes between theirs."

Lauren sniffed. "Yes, I suppose you're right. When I played the Coliseum and La Scala, we only performed three times a week."

"Yes, but then there were usually two operas playing," said Milly, getting Lauren's first costume ready. "You can't compare them. Now come along we need to get you ready."

"This is your fifteen-minute call, ladies and gentleman."

"Is it that time already?" said Lauren, sipping her drink. "Where does the time go to?"

Milly secured the wig cap on Lauren's head and placed the wig over it, using spirit gum to hold down the lace front, ready to apply the base makeup over it. Lauren's false eyelashes had been in place for nearly an hour and she loved using them when she talked, which reminded Milly of a pantomime cow she had once seen in a production of *Jack and the Beanstalk*.

"Lauren, I need to get you into this costume if you've a chance of making the first entrance on time."

"Yes, Milly dear," said Lauren, standing up. "These costumes are rather splendid, aren't they?"

"Yes," Milly agreed, pulling the gown across Lauren's shoulders and fastening the hooks. "Do try not to step on the train this afternoon. I had a heck of a job repairing the tear in it this morning."

"Oh, I am sorry my dear, I must remember to kick the train behind me when I turn."

Lauren made towards the door. "Wait a minute Lauren, you haven't got your dolly bag."

"How silly of me," said Lauren, taking the bag and making her way to the stage. She nodded at the other members of the cast who were also on their way to their positions.

"This is your five-minute call, ladies and gentleman. Overture and beginners please."

The orchestra was going through the under-stage entrance to the orchestra pit and began to tune up. There was a buzz from the audience as they made their way to their seats helped by the ushers. "Programmes," several called out "get your programmes here."

"Why are we going to the matinée?" asked Annie, following her daughter along the Golden Sands Pier.

"Because the evening performances were sold out; we were lucky to get these tickets."

"I say, they have done this pier up since we were last here, I don't remember this covered walkway."

"A fire destroyed it, don't you remember? It was in all the papers."

"Not in the *Weekly News*, it wasn't."

They were shown to their seats just as the lights dimmed and the orchestra struck the overture. Madge settled down to enjoy the show, hoping upon hope that her mother would do likewise. Normally, if her mother wasn't enjoying anything, she talked, but there was not a word to be heard and when the final scene of act one was finished, Annie turned to her daughter with a big smile.

"All those people in that parade, where did they all come from? That Lauren is quite funny, isn't she? I feel sorry for that Horace character."

"So, you are enjoying it," said Madge, a feeling of relief sweeping over her.

"I have to say, it's very good. Now you sit there and I'll go and get us both an ice cream."

Madge smiled to herself, her mother getting up to buy ice creams, that hadn't happened since she was a little girl."

When the curtain came down on the second act and the applause had died down, Annie was purely beside herself with joy. "I think I must have misjudged that Lauren Du Barrie, she was very good, very good indeed. I am so pleased we came."

Leading her mother out of the theatre, Madge felt triumphant and couldn't wait to tell them back home.

Lauren was back in her dressing room and Milly was helping her out of her finale costume. "They seemed like a good crowd this afternoon."

Lauren sighed. "Yes, they did, didn't they? I expect they appreciate watching professionals delivering their craft as only we know how."

Milly stifled a laugh.

Thursday 2 August

"Is anyone going to make a cuppa?" said Constance, as she began to apply her makeup, ready for that afternoon's performance. "I have a dreadful thirst today."

"It will be the kippers you had for breakfast," said William, brushing down his costume.

Sue Wilson stuck her head round the door. "I'll make some, Edith and Fred want one too, so I might as well make a big pot."

"Darling, you are an angel," said Constance. "If anyone fancies a chocolate digestive, I purchased some on the way in."

William lit a cigarette. "You know Constance, after seeing *Hello Dolly* I wonder we didn't try our hand at musical theatre."

"Perhaps the fact that neither of us can carry a tune in a bucket might be the answer there. Though I suppose we could have taken singing lessons, mother was always keen that I should, but I preferred the written text. I remember reading *A Midsummer's Night Dream* and thinking it was the most marvellous thing ever written."

"I enjoyed Dickens as a boy, though I did find them hard going," said William, remembering lying on the settee eating liquorice. "*Great Expectations* got me hooked and, after that, I couldn't get enough, I think I read *David Copperfield* next, happy days."

Edmund Green put his head round the door. "I say old chap, could I cadge a ciggie? left mine back at the digs and I'm gasping."

William offered him the packet. "Take one for later."

"That's awfully decent of you, old chap, I'll pay you back later."

"He is a nice young man," said Constance. "He should go far."

"Yes, I think you're right. He is always on the mark and his line delivery is exceptional."

"Oh, to be young again," said Constance with a sigh. "Oh, good, here's the tea."

Jack's voice came over the tannoy. "This is your 20-minute call."

"He is a treasure," said Constance, sipping her tea. "I am so pleased he decided to stay here instead of returning to the Sands. Such a gentleman and he remembered all of us when we arrived. Think of the theatres we have played, most hadn't a clue who we were."

"That's the business as it is nowadays," said William, enjoying his cigarette. "When we first started out doing rep it was all so different."

"Well, I suppose things change. But I am so pleased that Alfred Barton decided to try these productions, it has given us all a new lease of life. I hope they'll ask us back next year."

"Yes, it would be nice to keep all the gang together. It is fun when we all know each other so well."

"And not a bad egg among them," said Constance. "No bitchiness, it is a pleasure to work with this company."

William finished his cigarette and began getting ready.

Sue came back. "William, do me a favour and see if you can zip this dress up for me, it is playing havoc. I might need to run some candle wax over it when we come down this afternoon."

William obliged. "There you are my dear, you should ask Edith to take a look at the zip for you, she sorted out my trousers last season, had my fly-zip up and down as quickly as you like."

Sue laughed. "Can you hear him Constance, he needs locking up."

"I know Sue, dear," said Constance, adjusting her lipstick. "But no one will take him."

"This is your ten-minute call, ladies and gentleman, ten minutes to curtain up."

Constance got up from her dressing table. "I think I'll take Jack some biscuits. Is there any more tea in the pot, Sue?"

"Yes, there is. I'll pour another mug and take it to him."

"Hello Jack," said Constance. "I thought you would enjoy a chocolate digestive, Sue is bringing you some tea."

Jack looked pleased. "That's very kind of you Miss Anderson, I haven't been able to make a brew as yet, my kettle is on the blink."

"Then we must ask that nice Mr Barton to get you a new one," said Constance. "We're all going for a snack at the Teacake after the show if you fancy joining us, you'll have time before the variety show lot arrive."

"That is very kind of you, indeed. I would like to come along. It may have to be just for half an hour, though."

Constance picked up the telephone receiver on the desk and dialled. "Alfred Barton please, its Constance Anderson here. Yes, I'll hold, thank you.

"Alfred, Constance here, could you do me a big favour please and ask one of your staff to mind the backstage desk so that we can take Jack with us to the Toasted Teacake, he is such a dear and we would like to treat him. You're a darling, thank you so much." Constance replaced the receiver and smiled at Jack. "All sorted, there will be someone to take over when the curtain comes down and then you can relax and have a proper snack with us all."

Jack beamed. "Well, that really is so kind of you."

"Nonsense my dear man, you are a real gem and we all appreciate what you do for us."

"Best run, Miss Anderson. The curtain will be going up in two minutes."

Jack announced over the tannoy, "Two minutes to curtain, places everyone, two minutes to curtain."

Jack enjoyed poached eggs on toast and a lovely homemade ginger cake. The Clifftop Players made him feel he was one of the family. In all the years he had been doing this kind of work, this was the first time he had ever been included.

He thanked Pete from the hotel who had covered for him and was back at his desk in time to see the arrival of the variety artistes.

Jack Newbury, the comedian always passed the time of day, Miss Penny, as usual, was in a rush and was talking to herself, rehearsing an act in her head that she had done endless times before. Tom and Tilly always stopped for a quick chat before going to their dressing room. The Gaiety Girls all arrived in dribs and drabs, chatting to each other, and waving to Jack as they went by. Phil Yovell and Darren Yates arrived together clutching folders of music scores and last of all the top of the bill, Dean and Layla Dubrette arrived and gave a royal wave as they came through the stage door.

Jack always thought they were from another era, nice enough if you could get a word out of either of them, but they seemed to be living in some kind of dream world. He imagined them to have arrived in a horse drawn Hansom Cab, Layla in her white fur stole and tiara and Dean with a top hat and tails as if he had just come from high tea at The Ritz.

"Present for you," said Alfred, placing a boxed electric kettle on the desk. "I was under instructions from Constance Anderson to see it was delivered as soon as possible."

Jack laughed. "Thanks Mr Barton, it could have waited until tomorrow."

"You're doing a grand job, Jack. Everyone says so and we can't have you going without a cuppa," Alfred replied. "Now on

Saturday and Sunday evening I won't need you to do a night shift at the hotel, so I want you to have a couple of nights off. I can get Pete to cover the door for you he seemed to enjoy it this afternoon. Don't look so worried, it won't affect your wages, you are due to have paid holiday."

"Oh, that would be really nice" said Jack who did find his shifts tiring, but being the trouper that he was, never complained. "Thank you very much Mr Barton, much obliged I'm sure."

* * *

Saturday 4 August

As Madge helped her mother pack her suitcase she actually felt sorry to be going home. Perhaps they could repeat the experience again next year, but she knew better than to broach that subject just yet with her mother.

As they were checking out, the young man who had first checked them in was on duty and he smiled at them both. "Have you enjoyed your stay with us?"

Before Madge could answer, Annie said, "We have had a lovely time. Those rooms of yours are very comfortable and I appreciate the trouble of them being redecorated. What colour do you think they will be next year?"

"Oh, I couldn't possibly say. That would be the decision of our Executive Housekeeper. I understand that so many rooms are refurbished each year so that we keep up the high standard we set ourselves."

When they got into the car, Madge couldn't resist asking. "So, do I understand that we are coming back again next year?"

Annie looked at her daughter with a surprised look. "I would say so. I don't know why you would think otherwise."

Madge started the car.

"When I get back home," said Annie "I think I might refurbish the bedrooms, that dog's blanket in the spare room has seen better days."

Madge drove out of the carpark and smiled to herself.

* * *

"Another matinée darling," said Lauren, as she came through the stage door with Milly trailing behind her, carrying a costume that had needed repair for that afternoon's performance.

Several of the dancers were warming up doing leg stretches as Lauren went by. "Such dedication to the dance," expressed Lauren, glancing at them. "I don't think I could manage to get my leg that high, it looks very painful."

"Not if you are used to it," said Milly, following Lauren into the dressing room. "Now I have mentioned this before, kick the train behind you, I don't think this gown will stand another repair."

Lauren groaned. "Silly me, I always forget. Sorry Milly, I didn't mean to make extra work."

Milly made a face behind Lauren's back and hung up the offending item.

"Such a glorious day out there," said Lauren. "Did you see all those people on the beach? Hundreds of them!"

Milly nodded and went to fill the kettle.

On the stage Edwin and his staff were ensuring that everything was in place. They always carried out a sound and lighting check before each performance. The steam engine was standing off stage left, ready for its entrance and it looked quite frightening close-up, as if it were about to run off the tracks.

Some of the boys in the orchestra were going over a few bars of some of the numbers and tuning their instruments.

Several cast members were in and out of each other's dressing rooms, borrowing makeup and catching up on any gossip they might have missed.

Mona Buckle was checking that the auditorium was ready for the audience and paid special attention to the brass rails and was happy to find they were cleaned to her specification.

* * *

The following ~~week~~ day the musical continued with audiences ~~raving about the show but towards the end of the week,~~ Lauren had started to feel unwell. Milly had administered honey and lemon with aspirin, but it was clear that Lauren had a temperature. A doctor was called and after a full examination he said that Lauren had laryngitis, was totally run down and that she must rest.

"Oh my goodness," croaked Lauren. "What about the show?"

Milly made a call to Rita and she and June turned up to see the damage for themselves. It was clear that Lauren could barely speak and that she really didn't look well.

"We have no understudy as such," said June. "One of the dancers did learn some of the lines, but as we thought Lauren wouldn't be off at all, that didn't progress the way we had hoped."

Rita shook her head. "What are we going to do?"

"Could you do the part, Rita?"

"I'm sorry my old lover, I admit I do know the songs but as for the script, I haven't a clue."

"Lauren is going to be off for a least four performances or more," said June. "Milly relayed the doctor's instructions which we must take seriously. I have let Ray know and he is pulling his hair out, he was afraid something like this would happen."

"You have two alternatives," said Rita, thinking aloud. "You put on the dancer who at least knows some of the script, with the book in her hand or you have to pull the show until Lauren is well enough to return. As for Ray, I will have a word if you think that would help?"

Lauren, who was laying in her bed listening to this, groaned inwardly. She motioned to Milly to bring her some paper and a pen and scribbled a note, which she first showed to Milly and then handed it to June.

June read the note. "You mean put Milly on the stage as Dolly?"

Lauren nodded. Milly, who had kept quiet, stood up. "I know the part backwards and if I had a run through with the cast I think I could do it."

"But have you sung in public before?" queried June.

Milly burst into song and then recited a few of the lines of *Dolly* in an American accent.

Rita was amazed. "Well, June me old lover, Millicent Lansbury here may the answer to our prayers."

So, on Monday 6th August, with a very worried Ray Darnell in the theatre, the company were assembled at the Golden Sands and did a complete run-through with Milly as Dolly Levi. A set of costumes had been brought in from a theatrical costumer, though not in the same colour as Lauren's, but in keeping with the original production. As Milly sang and danced her way through the rehearsal without making one error, the whole company cheered and congratulated her. Notices were posted in the box office area and on the hoardings along the pier that due to the indisposition of Lauren Du Barrie, the part of Dolly Levi would be played by Millicent Lansbury until further notice.

Ray, who had trembled all the way through, collapsed in his seat as Rita did her best to fan him with her handbag. Jenny came along the aisle with a brandy.

"Pull yourself together, Ray. It is all going to be just fine," said Rita, rolling her eyes.

Ray took the brandy from Jenny and downed it in one. "I was so worried I can't tell you, I didn't know what to expect."

Rita slapped him on the back. "Well, me old lover, it has all come out well in the end."

That evening, Milly, with the help of Rita, renewed her makeup and put on the costume for the opening of the show.

Over the tannoy, the audience were informed, "Due to the indisposition of Miss Lauren Du Barrie, we are delighted to announce that the part of Dolly Levi will be played by Millicent Lansbury."

Several of the audience turned to each other asking who Millicent Lansbury was, no one had heard of her. From her first entrance through to the finale, Milly didn't put a foot wrong and the audience loved her. Word was out that although some were disappointed not to have seen Lauren, Millicent was a worthy replacement. A local newspaper reporter had been contacted to come and see the show and the local press, the following day, were telling the story of Millicent Lansbury's debut in a musical. A small photograph of Lauren in her sick bed was added for good measure and 'get well' wishes were expressed.

On reading the reviews, several locals were heading towards the theatre box office to see if they could obtain tickets only to be told that all houses were sold out.

Lauren, who was sad that she wasn't working, couldn't have been more pleased for Millicent and saw her in a different light. All those years that Milly had worked for her, she had never known of her hidden talent.

After the Wednesday matinee there was a knock on Milly's dressing room door and she was surprised and pleased to see that Jack, who had been the backstage doorkeeper at the Sands before the fire and was now working at The Little Playhouse, standing there with a large bouquet of flowers.

"Hello Milly," he said with a big grin.

"Oh, Jack, how lovely to see you," said Milly, beckoning him to come into the dressing room. "I have been meaning to come over and see you but I have been so busy."

Jack took off his hat. "I asked Mr Barton to give me the day off so I could come and see you and the show of course. My goodness, you were wonderful, not at all like the shy, retiring little thing I first met."

Milly grinned. "Oh, Jack I can't tell you how lovely it is to see you again," and she gave him a big hug.

"I hope you like the flowers."

"They are lovely, thank you so much. Have a seat and I'll organise some tea and cake."

"That would be grand," Jack replied, sitting down. "They have really done this old place up haven't they?"

Milly switched the kettle on. "They have indeed. When we have had some tea, I will give you a tour of the place."

"I wondered if you might allow me to take you out for a meal after the show this evening." Jack asked hopefully. "I am meeting some friends in town early evening and could come and collect you about ten-fifteen."

"Oh, that would be lovely. We could have a good old chin wag. I'll give Lauren a call to let her know I will be back late or she'll worry."

"How is she keeping? I heard she was unwell."

"She is getting better," said Milly handing a slice of Victoria sponge to Jack, "but you know Miss Du Barrie, it's the voice you know." And they both laughed.

Chapter Eight – August

A call to Rita from Sergeant York confirmed that there had been no further leads on Pamela. Rita thanked him for his time and told Jenny about the conversation she had had. The sergeant had been quite thorough in his enquiries and did his best to reassure Rita that there wasn't anything more to be done.

"It is best we put the baby to bed," she said. "It will not do me any good to pursue the matter further. I am sure that if there is anything to be learned, it will reveal itself in the fullness of time."

Jenny agreed, but she couldn't help wondering what was behind it all. On that subject, though, she decided it best to keep her own counsel.

On Friday 10 August, feeling slightly better, Lauren insisted that June take her to see *Hello Dolly*, she wanted to see Milly in action for herself. June had two seats allocated to her for every performance and a much dressed-down Lauren, with little makeup made her way along the row and sat down. Rita knew that Lauren was to be in the audience that evening but didn't tell Milly.

At the end of the performance, Lauren was in tears of joy and was escorted backstage to meet Milly.

Trying as best she could to speak, she sang Milly's praises until she started to cough.

Milly looked at Rita. "Rita, please organise some honey and lemon for Miss Du Barrie, it's the voice you know." Everyone looked at each other and smiled knowingly.

Jacob Manfred who was playing Horace Vandergelder congratulated Milly on her performance. "My dear lady, you are quite magnificent as I think Lauren here will concur. Never have I witnessed someone taking over a role as big as this in such a short time. I was concerned at first but you have proven my worries to be wrong. All the cast think you have done a sterling job. I feel honoured to be playing opposite you."

Milly was quite taken aback. "Thank you, Jacob. That means a great deal to me. I was afraid that they would cancel the show when Lauren couldn't go on and when I thought of all the hard work everyone had put into it, I felt I had to do something."

Jacob gave Milly a hug. "Thank you my dear, I hope we will have the opportunity of working together again."

Milly's dresser came into the room to retrieve costumes for pressing as Milly was removing her wig. It did feel strange sitting here taking off her make up but she smiled as she caught her reflection in the mirror, she wouldn't have missed it for the world.

The following week, Lauren returned to her role as Dolly, and Milly was once again her assistant. As Milly watched from the wings she could feel the excitement that she had felt when she was playing the role. Lauren was aware of the change in her assistant and trod more carefully than she normally did, for once. She became less demanding and chatted about things that she would normally not have bothered with.

June and Rita discussed Milly in some detail. "The girl is very talented," said Rita, "and it seems a shame to let that go to waste."

"She has had a good teacher," said June. "Lauren can be a bit of a madam, but her heart is in the right place. You know, Rita that I am planning to take this musical to Australia and I want Lauren to go with the show if she is willing."

"Oh, I'm sure she will be, she is familiar with the country, I remember her telling me about her appearances there."

"I am thinking of suggesting that Milly should be her understudy and maybe I could suggest that Lauren only plays six performances a week with Milly doing the other two, again if an agreement can be reached."

Rita thought for a moment. "I don't know how Lauren would feel about that."

"She has seen what Milly is capable of and, let's face facts, Lauren isn't in her first flush of youth. Having Milly beside her would take the pressure off."

Rita nodded in agreement. "When do you plan to mention it to her?"

"At this afternoon's matinee," said June. "Would you like to join me?"

"No, I don't think so. It may be best coming directly from you, I wouldn't want Lauren to feel she was being ganged up on."

So, that afternoon, half an hour before curtain, June spoke with Lauren and Milly. Milly kept quiet, showing no signs of any emotion.

Lauren turned from her dressing table. "Well, June my dear, I was thinking along the same lines. I do find eight shows a week somewhat tiring and I now know that someone who is very dear to me..." She turned and looked at Milly with a smile, "...is more than capable of delivering a performance to be proud of. If Milly is willing, then I think some kind of new contract should be drawn up and that the posters for Australia should state that, at certain performances, the part of Dolly will be played by Millicent Lansbury."

June smiled. "What do you think Milly? You are very quiet."

Milly smiled. "I would like that very much."

"The tour cannot start until next year," said June, "but by then Milly will have an Equity card and the necessary arrangements will be made. We will have to engage a new company as most of those here will not be able to go to Australia with you. But once the ball is rolling it should all turn out well."

June left the dressing room and Milly went over to Lauren. "Now, we must get your wig in place, it will be the five-minute call any time now."

Lauren took Milly's hand. "My dear Milly, thank you for everything and I mean that from the bottom of my heart. You have sacrificed a lot, working for me and I have truly appreciated it, though perhaps I haven't always shown it."

"This is your five-minute call."

Milly took the wig from its stand. "Now, Miss Du Barrie, we don't want you being late for your first entrance, people have paid good money to see you."

Lauren nodded, allowed Milly to put the wig on her head and followed her to the wings awaiting her entrance.

Donna Quinn dug her toes into the warm sand. She loved this sandy spot at Brokencliff-on-Sea, away from the hustle and bustle of the other beaches. Gorleston and Great Yarmouth would be packed with holidaymakers all making the most of the weather. She brushed some sand from her dress, adjusted her sunhat and leant back on the rock and heaved a happy sigh. From her bag she took her well-thumbed copy of *Twice Nightly* and opened it at the last page she had read. She felt safe in the world of the characters that had been created by her favourite author.

Life for Donna had changed since her introduction to Rita Ricer. With some outside help, she no longer felt the need to drink alcohol before she went on stage and instead found solace in a cup of tea or refreshing lemonade. She hadn't stopped drinking alcohol altogether, but knew her limitations. The odd couple of glasses were fine when she was in company, but drinking alone had become alien to her. Forgetting the dark days and nights that had blighted her life before, Donna felt that she had a second chance. Now she had regular bookings to look forward to throughout the week, leaving Monday and Tuesdays as well-earned days of rest. Wednesdays she played the Fisherman's, Thursday saw her at the Q Club in Norwich, Fridays the Trawlers Rest in Lowestoft and alternate Saturdays she played the Claremont Pier and The Hollywood Bar. Sundays she appeared at The George Borrow in Oulton Broad, lunchtime and evening, pulling in responsive audiences that the landlords appreciated. Thanks to the overwhelming support she had received, life was really good. She was able to explore new music, though she still included a couple of Italian ballads and a Patsy Cline in her playlist. She listened to the latest chart hits on the radio for anything that she could use.

She looked at her watch, it was coming up to 12.30 and she was feeling hungry and thought she might test the waters at The Toasted Teacake.

She finished the chapter and returned the book to her bag. She was alerted by the approach of a gentleman who had come down the stone steps to her right.

"Sorry, I didn't mean to startle you."

Donna smiled. "No harm done, I was just about to go and have some lunch."

"I have seen you before, haven't I?" the man said, smiling. "Aren't you Donna, the lady who sings at The Fisherman's?"

"Yes, as a matter of fact I am," replied Donna, basking in the compliment of being called a lady.

"I am Alfred Barton. I own the hotel here at Brokencliff. I caught the end of your act a few weeks ago."

Donna started to get to her feet and Alfred held out his hand. "Here, let me help you up."

Donna smiled. "Well I hope you enjoyed the act. They are a nice crowd in there."

"Look, forgive me for being forward, but you said you were going to have some lunch. I wonder if you would do me a favour and lunch with me in the hotel restaurant."

"That's very kind of you Mr Barton, but I hardly know you."

"But you will, if you have lunch with me. Look I'll be honest, I don't like lunching on my own and although I am

166

surrounded by staff all day, it doesn't do for the management and staff to mix socially."

Donna hesitated before answering. "I am sure your wife would be a good companion."

"My wife and I are divorced. Besides, she lives in Australia now. Look, I can see I've embarrassed you by my intrusion."

"No, it isn't that," replied Donna. "It's just that I don't very often get asked out to lunch."

"Well, then you should be." Alfred smiled. "Come on, what do you say?"

"Okay, you've twisted my arm Mr Barton."

"Call me Alfred please."

"Okay Alfred please." Donna laughed and followed him up to the parade above and then the short walk to the Beach Croft.

Stephen Price came forward as they entered the reception. "Good afternoon Mr Barton."

"Good afternoon Stephen, would you be as kind as to find me a table for two in the restaurant. Donna can I get you a drink from the bar?"

"Just an orange juice for me," replied Donna "I don't drink at lunchtimes and rarely anyway. I have to look after my vocal cords. They are my bread and butter."

"You won't mind if I have a small glass of vino?"

"Not at all," said Donna, removing her sunhat.

They were shown to their table and Alfred, who was feeling on top form, regaled Donna with the history of the hotel.

"And what about you Donna, has your career taken you to exciting places?"

Donna laughed. "Well, not so as you would notice, but things are certainly on the up. I have regular bookings through the week and I am hoping that my agent Rita will be able to fix me up with a couple of engagements in London in the not-too-distant future."

"Rita? you mean Rita Ricer?"

"Yes, I do."

"Rita is a friend of mine; a fine lady and she can spot talent a mile off. Of course, how stupid of me, I saw your audition at my theatre here. Rita interviewed you in this very hotel."

"I didn't like to mention it," said Donna sipping her orange juice as the waiter brought their starters. "I guess you meet so many different people, why would you remember little old me?"

Alfred looked at Donna. He had been quite taken with her on his initial sight of her all those weeks ago and now fate was lending a hand. Not one to push his luck, he hoped that as time went by, he and Donna would become better acquainted.

* * *

Donna had become something of a regular face at the Beach Croft and members of staff were noting that Alfred was always well-dressed when Donna came to call. Some had known his ex-wife Jean and wondered whether there was a romance blooming. Donna, who had curbed her drinking, was always pleased to see Alfred and they laughed and chattered through dinners and could also be seen taking the evening air together.

"There is no doubt," said Maud, putting her knitting to one side. "He is smitten."

"Well, it's nice to see him looking so happy, they do seem to be the perfect match," said Barbara.

"He has reserved tickets for them to see both plays and the show here; rumour has it he is also taking her to see *Hello Dolly*."

"I've tried to get tickets for that, but the box office says they are sold out."

"I am taking Enid, though I can't say she seems very enthusiastic. Couldn't get any comps the way we used to. I spoke with the lady running the box office, Selina, I think her name was, and she said that no complimentary tickets had been issued, with the exception of the opening night for the press and the local dignitaries. I bet the landladies were none too happy about that. They used to attend all the opening nights free of charge."

"Arh well Maud, things have changed since we were there with old Jim. This new company need to make the pier work and no doubt the cost of putting on *Hello Dolly* has set them back."

"You reminded me I must go and put some flowers on Jim and Karen's graves."

"You still do that then?"

"Always, Jim was a good mate to me over the years and Karen was a dear. I try to keep in touch with their daughter Debbie, but she and Peter are leading their own lives now. As you say Barbara, things have changed since the days of old Jim."

* * *

It was a Monday evening when Alfred accompanied Donna to see the variety show at The Little Playhouse. Alfred watched Donna's reaction to the various acts and after the final curtain had come down, he asked her what she thought of it.

Walking slowly back to the Beach Croft, Donna said that she thought the whole show was very good, she particularly enjoyed the dancers, thought the comedian Jack Newbury was very funny, she said she was still trying to work out how Tom and Tilly Mystery had done some of their tricks, Miss Penny's Puppets seemed a little out of place, but she did think that Dean and Layla Dubrette who topped the bill were a little dated in their choice of material.

"Well, it is such a small show and we try to cater for the various age groups it attracts."

"Do you book the acts?" asked Donna

"Well I have a say, but it is usually left to Rita's Angels to sort it all out. These acts are virtually unknown to many. It would cost a lot of money to put a big name on the bill we cannot compete with the theatre shows in Great Yarmouth."

"I suppose not," said Donna.

She followed Alfred into the hotel and he suggested a drink at the bar.

"I think I would be better going straight home," said Donna with a smile. "I am rehearsing some new material tomorrow morning and I need to be up and about early."

Alfred was disappointed. "Let me drive you home."

Donna shook her head. "I can ask reception to call me a taxi if that's okay with you."

"I can arrange that," said Alfred smiling back at her. "Don't forget we have a dinner date at the end of the week."

"Is that what we are doing then, dating?" she asked, looking him straight in the eyes.

Alfred blushed. "I would like to think so Donna, I have grown very fond of you."

It was Donna's turn to blush. "And I of you Alfred."

"I'll arrange the taxi," said Alfred. "We can wait in the lounge." But as he approached the reception to order the car, the receptionist said there was a taxi outside waiting and Alfred realised that his staff were one step ahead of him.

He escorted Donna to the car and held open the door for her, she looked up at him and then pulled him towards her. His reward was a light peck on the cheek and with that she was gone.

The summer season had been going well with blue skies and scores of holidaymakers arriving by train, coach and car. Joe Dean was delighted to know that every home at Finnegan's Wake had been booked solidly until to the middle of September.

Reverend Charles George, who had now vacated the vicarage, had taken rooms in Gorleston as a stop-gap until he had found a suitable property to purchase. A new vicar was in place at Brokencliff and Charles made himself available should Reverend Stephen Newman require any help. Martha Tidwell was none-too-happy with the new Reverend; he wasn't a patch on Reverend George and she made the appropriate noises whenever she thought anyone was listening. Reverend George told her that she must give Stephen time to settle in, but once Martha had taken a dislike to someone it was difficult to shift her.

Reverend Newman was unaware of his housekeeper's dislike for him and went about his parish business in much the same way as he had done in his previous location. He was always grateful for everything Martha did and commented on her excellent cooking ability, but even this cut no muster with the lady.

Phil Tidy found the new Reverend to be quite charming and was always pleased to see him when he called into the store. She had heard of Martha's gripes and one day, when Martha was in her store, she commented on how much she liked the new vicar to which Martha had groaned.

Phil was having none of it. "I have to say, Mrs Tidwell, you are very lucky to still be employed at the vicarage."

"How come?" asked Martha picking up a madeira cake from the shelf.

"Well many vicars insist on bringing their own housekeeper with them as they usually live in. I know that Reverend Newman's last housekeeper lived in and he was sorry to leave her behind, but when Reverend George had told him what a good housekeeper you were, he decided to leave things as they were."

Martha thought for a moment. "I could have found myself another position."

"And if you are so unhappy, you still could," said Phil, totalling up the bill for Martha. "But, remember, it may not be as convenient as the post you hold now. You would probably have to travel back and forth to goodness-knows-where and you wouldn't be able to pop home at the drop of a hat when the fancy took you."

Martha went bright red. "Well, when you put it like that…"

"That will be four pounds and 60 pence please Mrs Tidwell."

Martha handed over a five-pound note and put her groceries in her shopping bags.

"Thank you, then I'll be off," she said as she closed the shop door behind her.

"Have a good week," Phil called out after her with a smile. At that moment Dingle emerged from his sleep and trotted up to Phil. "I suppose you'll be wanting some doggie biscuits won't you? Come on then, let's see what I can find."

Joe Dean, who had his work cut out, was sorry when Charles said he had taken rooms in Gorleston; he wouldn't be able to see his friend as often. The caravan park, now reborn looked as if it was really going to take off and Joe felt he couldn't abandon it after it taken him so long to upgrade it. Charles felt quite sad too and would walk over to Brokencliff whenever he could, but he usually caught Joe in the middle of something and felt he was in the way.

However, one evening Charles had booked a table for the two of them at the Beach Croft and Joe made the effort to ensure he finished his day's work on time and met Charles for a pint in the Fisherman's. Sadie and Roberto always made them feel welcome and they took their drinks to a quiet corner of the bar. The juke box was playing gently in the background and one or two of the regulars were having a game of darts.

"Joe, I have to be honest, I don't enjoy living in digs and I am finding it difficult to find a location where I feel I can put some roots down," said Charles, supping his pint. "If I knew that you would be able to join me, it would make things so much easier."

Joe felt his stomach turn somersaults. "Charles, things are difficult for me at the moment, the park is just in its new infancy and I simply cannot abandon it."

Charles nodded. "Yes, I do see that."

"You know how much I like you, Charles but I cannot see a way forward at the moment. It may be best if we didn't make any joint plans, I don't want to mess you about."

Charles looked at his friend. "Let's not make any decisions yet, come on drink your pint and we'll walk over to the hotel. I know you have been working hard, a good meal is what you need, give you time to unwind."

Joe smiled and finished his drink. They put their glasses on the bar and waved goodnight to Sadie and Roberto.

"They make a nice couple," said Sadie.

Roberto laughed. "There you go again, match making, you'll never change."

"And you wouldn't want me to," said Sadie, rinsing some glasses in the sink. "But I am right about Alfred and our Donna."

"Well I haven't heard anything about an engagement."

"Give it time my love, give it time."

Charles and Joe were greeted by the head waiter who showed them to their table. The restaurant was quite busy.

"Have you heard how the new vicar is settling in?" said Joe, looking at the menu and finding it hard to decide.

"Stephen is getting on very well. I went along to his service last Sunday and the church was quite full. He gave a good sermon, I have to say. There were one or two people that aren't normally at church, so I think they must have gone along to check him out. I did notice that Martha Tidwell wasn't there, she doesn't approve of her new boss."

"I meant to go," said Joe, "but I was busy on Sunday morning and by the time the evening service came around I was too tired to bother. I am sure Mrs Tidwell will see the best side of him eventually, she probably doesn't like change."

"I think I'll have the soup to start, followed by the steak. I rather fancy a nice juicy steak," said Charles, summoning the waiter.

"I'll have the same," said Joe. He could never decide what to eat, even when he was at home.

"We'll also have a bottle of your finest dry white wine," said Charles with a smile to the waiter, who duly bowed his head.

"They are very well trained in here I must say," said Charles.

"Alfred will be pleased to hear that," said Joe.

"I'll be pleased to hear what?" said Alfred as he suddenly appeared at their table with a smile.

"Good evening Alfred," said Charles. "I was just saying to Joe how well trained your staff are."

Alfred beamed. "Thank you for saying that. I am very lucky to have a good set of staff and management and it's always pleasing when patrons recognise the hard work they all put in."

"Are you dining?"

"I am as a matter of fact I am just waiting for my guest. Oh, here she is now, Donna have you met the Reverend George, I think you know Joe."

Donna greeted them both and received a peck on the cheek from Alfred.

"And you must call me Charles my dear. I've dispensed with the collar. I like to think of myself as just one of the ordinary folk."

"I don't think there is anything ordinary about the folk of Brokencliff," said Alfred with a laugh. "Arh, here is your wine, enjoy your meal gentleman. Donna, our table is over in the bay window."

They waited until the waiter had poured the wine and departed.

"Well, there is certainly something going on there," said Joe. "They have been seeing quite a lot of each other and, I say, good for them. Some people are meant to be together."

Charles smiled at Joe. "Yes, Joe I think you are right about that, some people are meant to be together."

* * *

It was the last day of August and Lady Samantha was having coffee with her cousin, Lady Cora Sedgewick in the conservatory at Owlerton Hall.

"So how did the falconry displays work out in the end Samantha? Freddie and I had meant to come along and see it for ourselves, but we have been so busy this season."

"Well, I am happy to report that it turned out to be a great success and something we will continue with next year. The Hall has really begun to turn a profit. Even Harold is surprised about the turnaround in business."

Cora smiled. "I am so pleased for you. I was afraid that it would all become too much. These old places take a lot to keep them ticking over. I noted that the Sands was back in operation and I hear that the Playhouse here has been doing very good business."

"I believe Alfred Barton has turned that theatre around with some help, of course, from Rita Ricer."

Lady Cora coughed. "I was sorry to hear about Malcolm Farrow deserting her like that."

"My goodness, Cora you seem to be very up-to-date on the local gossip for someone who doesn't live in the area."

"I have my sources; besides I like to take an interest in these things."

"Malcolm Farrow was a charlatan," said Samantha with disgust, "and Rita deserves better. I think she is over the worst now, thank goodness."

"Do you know her well then?"

"We are acquainted and, I have to say I speak as I find, she is quite delightful company, down to earth and isn't afraid to call a spade a spade."

At that moment Penge entered and bowed his head. "I am sorry to interrupt your ladyship, but Mrs Yates would like to know what you require her to order from the butcher this week."

"Thank you, Penge. Tell Mrs Yates that I shall be down to see her in ten minutes."

"That's my cue to take my leave," said Lady Cora getting to her feet. "I am meeting with Janie McDonald this afternoon before returning home."

"I thought she was dead."

"So did a lot of people," said Cora with feeling. "After that shoplifting incident that landed her time in prison, she did try and keep out of the spotlight."

"Is she still with Beanie?"

"Oh no dear, he left her long ago, didn't like the scandal. She now lives in a one-up and one-down on the outskirts of Norwich. Like a rabbit hutch. I will take her out to eat, couldn't bear to be cooped up in that place."

The two ladies kissed each other on the cheek and as Lady Cora made her way out to the car park where Penge was waiting to see her to her car, Lady Samantha went in search of Mrs Yates who would either be elbow deep in pastry or in the pantry.

Chapter Nine – September

The summer season for the shows at The Little Playhouse and The Golden Sands was to come to an end on Saturday, 1 September and Alfred Barton had kicked his heels when he had realised that both theatres were to finish on the same date. He had a chat with Rita and then they got the variety artistes and the company of the plays together and asked if they would consider extending their run by an extra week so that they would close on the 8 September. Ray was consulted and the response was unanimous, no one had another job to go to, so Alfred took out a large advertisement in the local press stating that due to public demand the Little Playhouse was extended by an extra week.

"It's nice to be extended," said William to his wife. "I think this is the second only time we have ever been asked to stay on."

Constance smiled. "Say what you will about these plays of ours, they do attract a good crowd and people like a bit of light relief instead of all the heavy drama that is touring. Anyway darling, it means we can all go out as a company and enjoy the nightlife in Great Yarmouth. They are such a lovely company and spending playtime with them all is like being among family."

"Steady on Connie, you are getting quite sentimental in your old age."

* * *

Beverley had a brief meeting with Rita and confirmed that Harriet Fraser was working out very well. Beverley had spoken with Jill and Doreen in the Dancing School office and they were very happy with the cleaning. Jenny had said that she matched Mona Buckle's efficiency, but said it would never be right to say that in ear shot of Mona.

Beverley said she would speak with Harriet with a view to increasing her hourly rate and Rita gave her approval. "I shall leave it in your capable hands Beverley," she said with a smile. "You are doing a fine job."

* * *

Any hopes of extending *Hello Dolly* at the Sands were dampened as some of the company were already signed up to other productions and June Ashby realised, too late, that she had missed a trick. Auditions were already underway to recruit a cast for a proposed UK tour. To see an extended season at the Playhouse against her own, very expensively mounted musical annoyed her.

Rita was delighted for Alfred and could only soothe the nerves of June by stating that she had a possible UK tour to look forward to and hopefully an Australian run the following year.

"Well, news of the UK tour isn't good," said June. "It won't be happening, but Australia definitely will."

"Why no UK tour?" asked Rita.

"Well, theatres aren't available and some think that since *Hello Dolly* toured in the sixties, not enough time has lapsed. Mainly, though, it is finding the right theatres and locations. It will give Lauren some breathing space and also time to sort out visas and Equity membership for Milly. I need to get the ball rolling on that now."

June had been dropping her game somewhat and was so engrossed in sorting out problems with Roo productions that no further productions had been booked for the Sands, meaning that it would go dark.

Rita stepped in. "Look, me old lover, I can get together a variety show for the Sands to open at the end of September for a few weeks. All I have to do is make a few phone calls. There's a load of good acts on the books and I can get Bob in my London office to get onto it post haste. What do you say?"

June nodded gratefully. "Thanks Rita, it's my own fault, I hadn't looked further than *Hello Dolly*."

"We can run the show once nightly Monday through Saturday at 7.45. I will get onto it right away."

* * *

The closing night of *Hello Dolly* was something of a tear-stained affair. Lauren, who had enjoyed playing the part so much, was sorry to be taking a break from it and the company had all gelled so well that everyone was feeling a bit low.

The after-show party was well attended and everyone had a good time. Milly reflected on her moment in the spotlight and was looking forward to being the understudy and playing at least two performances a week on the tour of Australia.

Alfred was in attendance with Donna and in conversation with Rita, when Rita had an idea.

She motioned for Donna and Alfred to step outside the theatre bar to have a quiet word.

"I have something to put to you Donna," said Rita, smiling. "How would you like to appear at the Sands from the end of the month for a few weeks with a bill of other variety acts. I can't promise you top billing, but the money will be good and it is something that you will be able to put on your CV."

Alfred, who had been thinking along similar lines for his next season at the Playhouse, was secretly quaking inside. He had thought of offering Donna a season at the Playhouse and if she took this offer, it would stand her in good stead for the road ahead.

Donna was clearly stunned. "But I only play night clubs. I am not an experienced theatre artist."

"But you would be after this," said Rita. "All you would be doing is your own act and coming down with the rest of the company for the finale. You needn't do anything else. You could put together a 20-minute act with some of your favourite songs and there you go."

"Will you be directing this show?" Donna asked. "Only I heard you were stepping down."

"I will be stepping down next year but, in the meantime, I will be putting together this bill and I think the experience will do you good. You have seen how summer shows work; there is no magic to it. It is just a case of bringing together a variety of talent and entertaining an audience. We can organise some costumes for you from our extensive wardrobe if you would like."

"What do you say, Donna?" asked Alfred.

"'Yes please' is what I say," said Donna and Alfred squeezed her hand.

"And if you enjoy it," said Alfred, "I want to put you on the bill at the Playhouse next summer season, I've been meaning to say something to you, but this wonderful offer from Rita is just what the doctor ordered."

On the Monday morning at the office, Jenny had reflected on what Rita had told her.

"Well," she said, "you no sooner start to wind down than you wind yourself up again."

"Oh, it isn't so easy to just give it all up, as well you know with the Dancing School," said Rita. "I am showing Beverley the ropes and with help from the London office she will be at the helm by April next year, I shouldn't wonder."

"Did I hear my name mentioned?" said Beverley, coming into the office.

"Don't worry, me old lover, it was all good," said Rita. "By the way, I have this for you, it's a voucher from Alfred Barton for you and Ian to go and have a meal with two others of your choice at the hotel restaurant. I have a feeling he will be putting some work your way for next season."

Beverley smiled. "That is really kind of him. I will try and sort out a date with Ian and a couple of our friends."

"You know what they say Beverley, in this business there is no such thing as a free lunch."

"I'm beginning to realise that!" Beverley laughed as she left the office.

"How have you been getting on at the gift shop? Enjoying it?"

Jenny smiled "I have to say I have taken to it like a duck to water. Elsie has got a very nice lady, part-time who comes in on an ad-hoc basis and who used to work at Palmers, so she knows her way around a sale."

"Talking of sales, Palmers have an end-of-season sale on, why don't we go along and treat ourselves? Lunch is on you."

Jenny laughed. "Come on, I'll just let the girls know where I have gone."

"My dear friend," said Rita, grabbing her bag. "They don't need you holding their hands anymore. If they want you, they'll find you soon as not."

* * *

Muriel got into the passenger's seat of Freda's car. Since learning to drive, Freda had grown in confidence and now trips to the cash-and-carry no longer required a bus. Freda felt very happy behind the wheel of her car and even her husband Dick marvelled at the way his wife had taken to driving.

"It has been quite a busy season," said Muriel, offering Freda a boiled sweet as she started the engine.

"Well, it is a blessing that the Sands is up and running again, though I did think it was mean of them not giving us complimentary tickets for Dolly."

"Well, you can hardly blame them, besides Alfred Barton gave us comps to the Variety Show."

"They have extended that, haven't they? Business must be good."

"I have to say Freda, I thought that Joe Dean has done wonders with his caravan park, it looks really lovely."

Freda sighed. "Yes, there have certainly been a lot of improvements about the resorts. Even Owlerton Hall had a display of birds during the season. It turned out to be quite a big attraction, so I heard from Martha Tidwell."

"How is she getting on with that new Reverend of hers?" asked Muriel, taking a hanky from her bag.

"Well she doesn't like him very much, says he is not a patch on Reverend George. But as I said to her, you were always moaning about him, so you can't win."

Freda parked in the car park of Murdell and Pocock and grabbed her shopping bag from the boot. "Won't need too much in the way of groceries this week, I've only got two in."

Muriel followed her friend, not daring to mention that she was fully booked at her guest house until the end of the month. As they went around the warehouse of a store, they bumped into Lucinda who was singing - quite unlike her, they both thought – and, after passing the time of day, they carried on with their shopping.

"I have to say I didn't think Lucinda was looking very well," said Freda when they got back to the car.

"Funny you should say that, I had been thinking the same thing," Muriel replied. "I don't like to say too much, Lucinda can be very guarded when it comes to personal things, I just hope she is alright."

* * *

On Saturday, 8 September the final curtain came down on The Little Playhouse productions and retaining them for an extra week had paid off with 95% of the seats sold for all houses. Alfred was delighted. He invited all the company of players and variety acts to join him in a celebration of thanks at The Beach

Croft where a buffet, drinks and music had been laid on in the basement. There had been no refusals and it was nice to see both companies coming together, chatting and enjoying themselves. Rita was also in attendance with Jennie, Elsie, Jill Doreen, Beverley and Julie. Maud and Barbara had also been invited.

Three quarters of an hour into the party, Alfred took to the stage and made a speech.

"Ladies and gentlemen, performers, actors, actresses and theatre staff, I would like to thank you all for what has been a record-breaking summer season at The Little Playhouse. Box office receipts were up on last year and it is my hope that with all that is happening in Brokencliff at this time that we will be able to open our summer offering next year in June and run through to the second week of September. I have spoken with Ray Darnell and asked him to get as many of you back as he can for next year. With the variety show we will, of course be looking for a new bill, but I am pleased to say that the show you did this season can transfer to Clacton next year if you are all available."

There were murmurs of approval from the assembled crowd.

Rita's Angels who put the variety bill together will be in touch with you to see what your availability is like. As some of you may have heard, Rita will be taking a back seat next year and Beverley, who I know you have all met, will be taking over the reins of the agency."

There was a huge round of applause.

"May I take this opportunity to wish you all continued success" Alfred continued "And thank you all once again from the bottom of my heart. You are the best!"

Just as he was about to leave the microphone, Alfred was handed a piece of paper by Minnie Cooper who hurried to attract his attention.

"Ladies and gentleman, there has been a call from Ray with some rather exciting news. As you are aware *Wardrobe Doors* went on tour and was a great success, even though it didn't have any of the present company in it. Ray has been approached by the BBC to film the play and show it on national television. He would very much like the original company to return here in November and the beginning of December to play again. The BBC will film at least two performances from different angles. The Playhouse is quite small as you will all know, so the filmed performances will have a smaller audience than usual. Ray would like to know if you would all be willing to do this."

Alfred looked out at the company and got the thumbs up from all the rep company.

Murmurs went around the room with everyone delighted by the news.

"He does make a lovely speech," said Constance to Layla Dubrette, who was standing nearby.

Layla smiled. "Yes, he is quite a charming man. Dean and I have been most happy working at the theatre; it has a special magic all of its own."

Constance nodded "Yes there is something about the old place. I shall look forward to coming back later in the year and next year too."

"I suppose you will have new plays to work with," said Layla taking an interest.

"Oh yes, I expect so."

"Dean and I came in and watched both your productions and were much impressed. There is an art to delivering a good farce or comedy."

"Thank you for saying so," said Constance.

"You should have seen *Wardrobe Doors*," said William interrupting the pair. "It was a hoot and Constance here was hit on the head by a flying door knob every performance. Now the whole country will see it thanks to the BBC."

Constance groaned. "Don't remind me."

"Oh, do tell," said Layla. "Look, there is a vacant seat over there, let's go and have a proper chat."

* * *

It was with a stroke of luck that Bob Scott was able to secure a top of the bill for the Sands in the shape of Eddie Carroll who had appeared in several variety shows and was well known up north. The JB Dancing School managed to pull together four male and six female dancers. Rita had found that comedian Charlton Ray was available; she had seen him perform many times and he had been a great pal of her late husband Ted. Beverley contacted a speciality act, The Foremans who juggled and did a balancing act on a pole, and had also secured Mary's Marionettes, an act that featured five-foot puppets that were life-like and, with Donna Quinn the bill was complete.

Rita had been in touch with Maurice Beeney who agreed, as it was Rita asking, to get his All Rounders Orchestra out of retirement and provide the necessary music accompaniment. Rehearsals were to take place on Thursday, 20th September and the show would open for three weeks from Monday, 24th

September. When Donna saw her name on the posters around Norfolk, she trembled with excitement and was looking forward to being part of it.

THE GOLDEN SANDS THEATRE
GREAT YARMOUTH

Rita Ricer for Roo Productions presents

"AT THE END OF THE PIER"
A Variety Show for Three Weeks from Monday 24th September featuring

"EDDIE CARROLL"
The Man with a Song in his Heart

Comedian - Charlton Ray
"I'm Watching You Missus"

The Foremans
Juggling and Jinks on a Pole

The Fabulous
Mary's Marionettes

The JB Showtime Dancers
Choreography – Jenny Benjamin

And Special Guest Appearance of Singing Sensation
Donna Quinn

The All Rounders Orchestra under the direction of Maurice Beeney

Nightly at 7.45 Monday – Saturday
Special Matinee performances Wednesday and Saturday at 4.00

STALLS - £3.00 - £2.00 and £1.00
DRESS CIRCLE - £3.00 and £2.00
Bookable in advance at the Theatre Box Office

On the day of rehearsal, everyone was assembled in the theatre at nine am promptly. Maurice and his boys were set up in the orchestra pit, Jenny was giving last-minute instructions to the dancers and Rita was standing at the front of the stalls, armed with a folder containing the running sheets.

Mona Buckle had sneaked into the back of the auditorium to get a glimpse of what was taking place and thought to herself that it was quite like the old days.

Rita watched Jenny and smiled to herself; Jenny had wanted to choreograph this show and as Jill and Doreen were busy working on other productions she had got her wish. She had discarded her old routines and had worked out some new ones and it seemed that as she had been away from it so long, the new ideas came to her easily.

"Right everyone," said Rita. "Clear the stage please and be ready to do your act at the appropriate time. Edwin are your backstage boys ready?"

Edwin walked on from the wings and waved at Rita. "All ready and raring to go," he called.

Maurice Beeney raised his baton and the orchestra struck up the overture, a medley of some of the numbers that were to be used in the show.

The curtain rose and the JB Showtime Dancers were "Putting on the Ritz" in high, top-hat fashion in some dazzling costumes. Rita was much impressed, Jenny stood next to her hoping everyone would keep in step; she had no worries, they were all spot on.

Then Charlton Ray entered and told a few jokes before introducing The Foremans, whose act had Jenny gripping Rita's arm in anticipation of what might happen. Charlton returned to the stage to do his own act, followed by another routine from the dancers who then introduced Donna Quinn who brought the first half of the show to a close with a medley of Patsy Cline songs and two ballads.

"Well, everything is running very smoothly and to time," said Rita, much impressed. Unbeknown to her the company had rehearsed together at a local hall, knowing that Rita liked perfection and they didn't want to let her down; even Jenny hadn't been in on the secret.

The second half opened with another dance routine, involving some particularly spectacular moves by The Foremans, Charlton returned to the stage for a couple of well-placed gags and then Mary's Marionettes featured.

Mary, with three puppeteers, presented a galaxy of pop stars in puppet form including Sandie Shaw, The Beatles, Adam Faith, Cilla Black, Dusty Springfield, Gene Pitney and Shirley Bassey.

Rita was delighted, knowing the audiences would love them. Then the dancers returned to introduce the top of the bill Eddie Carroll, whose voice filled the theatre with songs of love and romance. Rita handed Jenny a handkerchief as she had been reduced to tears. The grand finale followed with the dancers in yet another routine introducing the entire company to say goodnight.

The curtain came down and then raised again where it remained as Rita and Jenny made their way onto the stage.

"Well, I have to say that is the best rehearsal I have ever seen in all the years I have been in the business. The audiences are in for a rare end-of-summer treat. I am to understand that an article about the show will appear in tomorrow's *Great Yarmouth Mercury*. The box office has reported that the bookings are very healthy indeed and we have large coach parties booked from across the Norfolk and Suffolk areas.

"Maurice, I must say a big 'thank you' to you and the boys; the orchestrations were wonderful."

Maurice was truly delighted and the company on the stage gave a hearty round of applause.

"Now, I happen to know that tonight reservations have been made for you all to enjoy a meal at The Star Hotel, courtesy of Roo productions. Please arrive by seven for a 7:30 sit-down."

This was met with appreciative murmurs.

"I suggest that you all enjoy the few days off and be back in the theatre by three on Monday afternoon, when we can run through anything you would like to again. We will serve a light tea in the theatre bar from 5:30 for those of you that would like to partake."

One of the dancers stepped forward, a young man named Billy. "I would just like to say a big 'thank you', on behalf of all the dancers here, to Jenny Benjamin who I know at short notice came out of retirement to put us through our paces."

There was a big cheer from the assembled company.

Jenny was moved and thanked everyone.

As they all went to their dressing rooms to change, Rita took Jenny by the arm. "Do you remember 1969 when I walked into this theatre and had a pop at Don Stevens?"

"Like it was yesterday," Jenny replied. "He really laid into me as I remember, but his heart was in the right place."

"Come on, old dear, why don't you and I take a stroll on the promenade, have a light lunch in one of the restaurants in Regent

Road and take the rest of the day off? Beverley is running the office and doesn't expect me back."

"What a good idea," said Jenny, following Rita up the theatre aisle to the exit.

Mona walked forward and greeted the pair. "I have to say, Mrs Ricer, that show was first class, first class indeed."

Rita thanked her. Any praise from Mona Buckle was praise indeed.

The sun was shining as they walked out on the pier and slowly strolled along, taking in the scene on either side of them. The covered walkway was going to prove a bonus when the nights turned colder and audiences made their way to the theatre.

"You know that June is thinking of putting on a pantomime at Christmas?" said Jenny.

"Oh Lord, no!" exclaimed Rita. "That won't go down well with the amateur groups, that's their bread and butter."

"Perhaps we can point her in the direction of a Christmas show like the one you did, summer season, at the Nest last year."

The mention of the Sparrow's Nest reminded Rita of Malcolm, but she swallowed hard and let the thought go, that baby had since been put to bed.

"Look! Joyland is open," said Jenny. "Let's have a ride on the snails." And, taking Rita by the arm, she dragged her into the small funfair, laughing.

* * *

The show opened and there was wasn't an empty seat in the auditorium. Muriel and Freda had managed to book some seats at the front of the stalls and a few rows back was Lucinda with two of her regulars, George and Dinah Sergeant who had returned for another break. Mona Buckle had come along and sat on an aisle seat in her finery, which had become something of a feature. She was asked by the gentleman seated behind her to remove her hat as he found the peacock feathers distracting.

Mona removed the offending item and felt quite lost without it, hats were her thing.

Freda had actually turned up in something rather nice, which made a change from some of her creations, and Muriel thought how smart she looked. However, she was let down by her choice of perfume, yet another bottle from her man with the suitcase on the market. This one was called 'Lingering' and as the evening went on it certainly lived up to its name. Several people in the audience turned to the person next to them with a sniff. Muriel, ever the smart one, kept a handkerchief handy sprinkled with lavender water.

The reviews for the show in the local press the following day were glowing. There was praise for the entire company with special mention of the excellent dancers and quality of the acts. 'No second-rate artists here' one headline read. Donna Quinn came in for exceptional praise and, according to one critic, "a star had been born".

It was all very flattering and pleasant to read some nice articles.

"Which only goes to prove," said Rita, "you can spend months putting a show together and then you take about ten minutes on another, and it comes up trumps all the way."

There were queues at the box office and the show looked like being a sell-out.

"Another week do you think?" asked June to Rita.

"Why not, let's put it to the company." They did and the company said 'yes', so for the second time in a season a notice went into the press that due to popular demand the show was to be retained for a further week.

* * *

"So, Miss Haines, I have the results of your hospital tests," said Doctor Munroe. He took off his glasses and laid them on his desk. "I am afraid the results are what I feared. The cancer has spread considerably, if only you had come to me sooner."

Lucinda showed no emotion. "I guessed something wasn't right over a year ago, but I was so busy with GAGGA and all the other things going on that I didn't act as quickly as I might have."

"You see, my dear there is little I can offer you in the way of treatment. I can give you some strong pain relief and I would emphasise that you must attend the clinic regularly so they can keep an eye on things."

The thought of going back and forth to The Norfolk and Norwich didn't fill Lucinda with any hope at all. "How long do you think I have got?"

"It is difficult to say," said Doctor Munroe being as gentle as he could be. "You may have another year, but what I would advise you to do is make sure that you have everything in place."

"You mean making sure I have written a will?" said Lucinda. "Putting my house in order, that sort of thing."

The doctor nodded. "Is there anyone you can tell? A friend, perhaps."

Lucinda thought of Muriel, who over the months they had worked together, she regarded as the closest person to her. "There is someone but I don't know if I could burden her with it."

"You could try," said the doctor. "It is always worth having a friend on your side. When things get too bad you will, of course, be admitted to hospital."

"Oh, I wouldn't want to die in a hospital bed," said Lucinda, shuddering at the mere thought.

"Then speak to your friend, maybe he or she will be able to help you prepare when the time comes."

The doctor shook hands with Lucinda and watched as this brave lady, showing no fear or upset, left his office. Breaking such news was part of his job, but one he didn't enjoy.

Chapter Ten – October

M aud put down her knitting and looked over at her sister, Enid who was struggling with a crossword. "I think we should have a few days away. These October days are getting me down. There is nothing doing at the Little Playhouse as it's being decorated and I always feel a bit low this time of the year."

Enid looked up from her puzzle. "What's another word for leave out – four letters?"

"Omit," replied Maud. "Now, how do you feel about going away?"

"Where had you in mind?"

"Not too sure, I think I will pop along to Jolly Travels and see what they have on offer."

"Nowhere foreign," said Enid, looking over her spectacles.

"I will see what I can do. Let's face it love, the last time we went anywhere foreign was Grimsby," replied Maud with a laugh and getting up from her chair. "Five nights should do it, change of scenery, it will do us both the world of good."

Tara Conner looked up and smiled at Maud as she entered Jolly Travels. "Good morning madam, how can I help you?"

"Well," said Maud, pulling up a chair in front of Tara's desk. "My sister and I would like to have five nights away somewhere, what can you recommend?"

"Have you thought of Norwich?" asked Tara with a smile. "Full of history, the cathedral is something to die for and if you enjoy taxidermy, the castle is full of stuffed beasts from all over the world."

"But Norwich is only 20 miles away and I can go over there anytime I choose."

Tara smiled again and pulled open her desk drawer. "Let's see what I can find in my brochures. I suppose Blackpool is out?"

"A bit like taking a busman's holiday?" said Maud.

"Do busmen take lots of holidays then?" asked Tara with a look of concern, "I bet that doesn't please the bus companies."

"I really have no idea what their holiday entitlement is. All I am concerned with at the moment is booking five nights away for my sister and I."

Tara spread a map of the United Kingdom across the desk. "How about Canterbury?" she said, pointing.

"That's Preston," said Maud, unimpressed. "Canterbury is down here in Kent."

"Is it?" said Tara "Have they moved it, I could have sworn it was up here."

"Have you been doing this job long?" Maud enquired, trying not to lose her patience.

"This is my second week and Mr Romsey said I could work on my own today, its Mo's day off and he has gone for an early lunch."

"What does your brochure recommend?"

Tara opened the brochure and looked at the sheet of paper Mr Romsey had given her advising her to push a couple of slow burners.

"There's a coach trip to Bournemouth for six days that is all inclusive of hotel and meals," said Tara, pointing on the map to Wales.

Maud shook her head. "Nowhere coastal. Haven't you got something inland?"

"You mean nowhere near the sea?" said Tara, looking at Maud who was nodding her head frantically. Tara looked at the map again. "Well there is lots of sea, so there must be lots of places not beside the sea."

Maud rolled her eyes and tutted.

"What about Clifton? It's near Bristol," said Tara pointing on the map again.

"That is Hunstanton," said Maud, stabbing the map with her index finger. "That is Bristol over there and there is Clifton just above it."

"Oh, I am sorry," said Tara with a giggle. "I wasn't very geographical at school. In fact, I sometimes catch the wrong bus home, I have no sense of direction, and it took me a week to find the correct way to the office."

"Where do you live then?"

"Acle."

"But that's only a short train ride away."

"Not if you come on the bus," said Tara. "So how about Clifton? The hotel looks very nice from the photographs, it's the Clifftop Regal. All the rooms have their own bathroom which is quite a unique feature, the hotel is in its own grounds with stunning views of Clifton and you are only a short walk from Bristol, it says here. You travel by coach, so it's a door-to-door drop off. It is booking quite quickly so you would need to snap it up if you want to take advantage of the special rate."

"When is it for?"

"Two weeks tomorrow, leaves on the Monday morning at 9:30 and returns on the following Saturday morning from the hotel at ten." Tara slid a piece of paper across the desk with some prices on it. "There is a five per cent discount on those prices if you book today."

Maud, who was getting a bit fed up with the inefficiency, managed to smile and looked at the prices. "Well that does seem very reasonable, we'll take it."

Tara got out her booking pad and began to take down some details. She then telephoned the hotel in question to reserve the twin room for Maud and her sister.

"Hello is that The Regal Clifton? Oh, hello this is Tara from Jolly Travels in Great Yarmouth; I think I spoke to you the other day. Yes, Janet I remember your voice, how is your mother now? Did her complaint clear up? Oh, I know, that can be very nasty, my aunt suffered with it something chronic, she was never the same after that, couldn't use rubber gloves any more, said they brought her hands out in a rash. Anyway Janet, I want to make a booking for the special, a twin room please with a nice view, yeah like we booked the other day."

Maud coughed.

"So that's five nights on receipt number 4976. Thanks ever so much Janet, bye for now."

Tara smiled at Maud. "That's the hotel taken care of now let me write out the tickets for the coach."

Maud, who had been to the bank beforehand, was able to pay in full. Tara thanked Maud for her booking and wished her a happy holiday. Just as Maud left the agency Mr Romsey walked in. "Everything okay, Tara?"

"Oh yes, Mr Romsey. I have just done my first booking for Clifton."

"Well done, the Clifftop Regal?"

Tara nodded.

"How many have we going on that particular excursion?"

Tara looked in the register. "With that lady and her sister, it makes six people."

Mr Romsey sighed. "Best phone the coach company and ask them to supply a smaller coach, no point in a 56-seater turning up."

"Yes, Mr Romsey," said Tara picking up the receiver and dialling. She heard the voice of one of the operators of Cosy Cox Coaches; it was Emma, who Tara knew quite well and they had a little chat before getting down to the business in hand.

"Did she really? Oh, that's quite exciting isn't it and with a greyhound you say. Oh, I would have liked to have seen that."

When Maud reached home, she looked at the tickets she had been given about Cosy Cox Coaches and read the information inside to ensure she was fully aware of the pickup point and the time of departure. She hoped Enid would be pleased with her choice.

Tara Connor put on her coat, picked up her bag and said goodnight to Mr Romsey. She headed for the bus stop and was pleased to see the bus coming. She found her usual seat and reflected on her day at the office. All in all, she thought, she was making progress and the money coming in certainly helped.

An hour later, the bus arrived in Acle and she headed off down the lane to the family home, a small farm holding that over the years had reduced in size. She greeted her father, Matty, who was sitting beside the hob with his pipe.

"Hello my girl, you had a good day then?" he asked in his raspy tones.

"I did, Dad," smiled Tara. "I think my boss is quite pleased with my work, so as long as it continues, I won't have to go back to waiting at tables."

Tara had previously worked at a small restaurant in Great Yarmouth but had never been happy there; the staff had been stand-offish and she had felt that she had never fitted in.

"I'll make some tea and take one up to Mum. I've got some chops, so we can have them with some mash, carrots and peas."

"That sounds champion," replied her father. "Old Albert has been sorting out the top field and young Jake has made headway with the barn. The cows are going to market next week, so I hope we make a good price."

Tara smiled at her father's optimism, she knew in her heart of hearts that the cows wouldn't fetch much, but every penny counted and without the help from Albert and Jake, the farm would have gone to ruin some years ago. Albert Smith lived in a small cottage on the land and Jake came in from the village and worked for a small wage and could take some of the fresh produce home to his mother. He also worked at a garage which kept him busy as a mechanic and so helping out on the farm wasn't a regular occurrence. But he liked the Connor family and liked to do what he could to help.

Tara poured out a mug of tea for her father, took a cup and saucer from the cupboard and poured one for her mother.

Her mother was propped in bed, a magazine lay to one side of her and she smiled as Tara came into the bedroom.

"Hello Mum, how are feeling today? Did Elsie come in and see you."

Her mother nodded. "Elsie came with them flowers and some grapes. She said she was going to bake some meat pies tomorrow and would bring one over for us, so you won't need to do a shop tomorrow."

Tara put the cup and saucer down on the bedside cabinet. "That's really kind of her. I've got some chops for our tea tonight; do you think you will be able to manage the stairs and come down to the kitchen?"

"My leg has been playing me up and I'm feeling a bit tired, to tell you the truth. Doctor is coming tomorrow so I hope he can give me something."

Tara kissed her mum on the cheek. "I'll go and get started on the chops then and bring yours up on a tray." As Tara descended the steep staircase, she knew that it would take more than a visit from the doctor to make her mum well again.

As she was dishing up the dinner, Jake popped his head around the kitchen door. "Hello beautiful."

"Hello beautiful yourself Jake Harris, what can I do for you?"

"There's a dance over Martham way on Saturday night and I wondered if you would like to come along with me."

Tara smiled. "And how do suppose we are going to get over to Martham?"

"Your dad said I could borrow the truck."

"I'll have to think about it," said Tara coyly.

"Well don't you be thinking too long, there are other girls I could ask."

Tara blushed. "I'm sure there is, Jake Harris."

"But none as beautiful as you, Tara."

"Oh, be getting on with you, you'll have me all of a doodah."

Jake grinned. "You can tell me tomorrow." And with that he shouted goodnight to Mr Connor and left.

"Was that young Jake I could hear?" asked her mother as Tara put the tray down in front of her.

"Yes, it was. He's asked me to a dance on Saturday. Dad said he could borrow the truck."

"Then you should go, it would do you good. Jake Harris is a fine young man and he'd be lucky to have you on his arm. He holds down a steady job at the garage and comes here when he can to help out and there aren't too many men like that about."

"Thanks Mum, but I have really nothing suitable to wear."

"What about that lovely gingham frock, you look a fair treat in that."

"Oh, that old thing."

"Now I know you don't like the thought of it, but have a look in your sister's wardrobe, there are plenty of things in there that would fit you."

"But it don't seem right" said Tara looking perplexed.

"Janice has been dead two years now, Tara and there is no good dwelling on it. She would be happy to know that you were wearing one of her dresses. That's why I haven't had the heart to clear out her things. Best they go to you rather than the jumble sale."

"I'll think about it. I'll go and see if Dad wants another cup of tea."

Mary Connor wiped a tear from her eye and began to eat her dinner. Tara had always been the stronger twin and it pained her to know that Janice had inherited bad health from her side of the

204

family. She was grateful that Tara had shown none of the symptoms and prayed that it would always be so.

Saturday night came around and Tara had chosen a fifties-style frock of her late sister's. "Will this do, Mum?" she asked, giving a twirl.

"You look lovely," said her mother, remembering the first time she had seen Janice wearing it. "You'll need a coat; it might turn cold later."

"I've got my black mac," said Tara. "It should keep out the cold and I'm not sure whether the heating in the van is working."

Her mother smiled. "I am sure Jake will have a blanket to put over your knees. You have a lovely time and ask your dad to pop up and see me. There is something I want to talk to him about."

Tara kissed her mother and went downstairs just as she heard the toot of a car horn.

"That'll be Jake," said Tara, kissing her father on the cheek. "I won't be late, Dad and Mum says will you go up and see her please."

Matty Connor smiled at his daughter and gave her a couple of pounds. "Get yourself and Jake a drink on me and don't overdo it."

"Thanks Dad. Don't worry about Jake, he will have a couple of shandies; he says it isn't right to drink and drive."

"That boy has got a good head on his shoulders," said Matty getting up from his chair. "I'll take your mum a cup of tea. You have a lovely time my girl."

As Tara approached the truck, Jake came around the side and opened the door for her. "You look lovely," he said and gave a whistle.

Tara smiled happily. "I do my best."

The evening passed in a pleasant way, Jake was very attentive and Tara who always felt safe in his hands allowed herself to enjoy dancing. True to form, Jake had a couple of shandies and Tara had one gin-and-tonic and then moved onto orange juice.

When Jake pulled in beside the Connor Farm he turned to Tara. "I've been thinking."

"Oh, you don't want to do too much of that, it will rot your brain."

"Hush now, I'm being serious. Tara how would you feel about us getting engaged?"

In the dark, Jake couldn't see the reaction on Tara's face. "You mean engaged to be married?"

"Well yes," said Jake "I think that's the normal way of things."

"You mean with a ring and all that."

"Of course I do, I just thought I ought to ask you first before I go and speak to your father."

"Oh my goodness!" exclaimed Tara. "Yes please, Jake Harris, yes please."

"Well you'd better give me a kiss then."

Tara leaned towards Jake and kissed him. "Oh, I can't wait to tell me mum, she'll be so excited."

Jake gave Tara a hug. "Well you'd better get yourself inside, I'll return the truck tomorrow and then I can cycle to the garage."

"Night then," said Tara.

Jake watched as Tara walked down the pathway to her front door, the porch light was on and then he started up the engine and drove home feeling very happy indeed.

* * *

Two weeks later with their cases packed Enid and Maud were ready for their holiday.

"This appears to be our coach," said Enid looking behind her at Maud who was struggling with two suitcases.

On the side of the coach was the name Cosy Cox Coaches and the slogan, "Go all the way with our friendly drivers."

Maud spotted it and took a sharp intake of breath.

The driver was standing at the door of the coach and smiled at them both. "Let me put your luggage in the hold."

"Thank you," said Maud. "I am Maud and this is my sister Enid."

"Oh yes," the man replied. "You are both on my list.

"And what shall we call you?"

"You can call me Andrew."

"Andrew is a nice name," said Enid with a smile.

"It isn't actually my name, but everyone calls me Andrew."

"So, what is your name, love?" said Maud, following her sister onto the coach.

"Andy," said the driver.

"Maud lowered her voice. "Oh great, this is going to be fun."

But the fun had only just begun; seated on the coach were Freda and Dick Boggis with Muriel and Barry Evans.

"Well, that's the lot," said Andrew, addressing the six passengers. "We will be leaving for Clifton in five minutes, with two stop-off breaks for a cuppa and the usual."

Maud smiled at the others and motioned Enid to go with her to the back of the coach.

"Enid likes to sit at the back," she said, by way of explanation, "as she thinks she gets a longer ride."

"Well," called out Freda, "that's what my old mum used to say and we used to laugh, didn't we Dick?"

Dick, who was tucking into a bag of crisps, mumbled that they did.

"Is that a new aftershave you are wearing, Dick?" asked Muriel, as a strange aroma reached her nostrils.

"Yes, it is," said Freda, answering for him. "It's the new aftershave for men, I got it off the bloke on the market."

"It's rather pungent," said Muriel getting up to open a window. "What's it called?"

"Knobbit," replied Freda, "for men who know where they're going."

Maud who had overheard the conversation whispered to Enid, "Clifton by all accounts, oh I do hope they won't be staying at the same hotel as us, can you imagine it?"

"I'd rather not," replied Enid. "Want a mint?"

Maud took a mint and, as the coach started up, settled down to enjoy what she hoped would be a lovely ride to their destination.

Maud was horrified to learn that their rooms were next to Freda and Dick, with Muriel and Barry on the other side.

The room was pleasant enough, though Enid thought that the décor needed updating and the two paintings of sheep that hung on the wall were hardly what one would have expected.

The bathroom was nearly as large as the bedroom area, so there was plenty of space to spread out. Once they had unpacked, the two sisters decided to go to the hotel bar and have a drink before going in for the evening meal. The barman introduced himself as Eric, served them with two schooners of sweet sherry and they sat down near the large picture window. The daylight was fading so it was difficult to see anything, but both felt a little jaded from their coach trip so sat quietly and enjoyed their drinks.

Fifteen minutes later they went into the restaurant and were seated in a bay window recess which felt quite cosy. It was apparent that their travelling companions had not booked full board as they didn't appear for a meal. Maud heaved a sigh of relief; at least they would be spared making small talk. She checked the times when breakfast was served and suggested to Enid that they should get up early so as to avoid seeing the other four, she guessed correctly that Freda and Dick wouldn't be early risers and the chances were that Muriel and Barry would follow suit.

The three-course meal consisted of oxtail soup or grapefruit juice, followed by roast beef or chicken served with vegetables and roast potatoes and, to finish, a choice of four sweets or cheese-and-biscuits.

They finished their meal and returned to the bar where they both enjoyed a pot of tea, then retired to the bedroom where Maud was eager to continue her Agatha Christie mystery and Enid her crossword puzzle.

The break did the sisters the world of good and they were able to visit the Bristol dockland area, marvel at some of the museums and enjoy a trip to Bristol Zoo and all without bumping into the landladies. They had passed them a couple of times in the hotel and exchanged pleasantries but had kept their itinerary to themselves, never revealing where they were off to.

Returning on the coach to Great Yarmouth, it appeared that the landladies' party had done very little, though a trip to the zoo had been mentioned with Freda saying how much see had enjoyed seeing the elephants and also spotting Johnnie Morris who was filming on the day they were there. Freda had tried to get into the shot hoping to appear on Animal Magic, but the llama that Johnnie was with at the time had other ideas and the camera crew ensured that Freda was kept well away.

"I mean, that's all you want," said Enid, handing her sister a toffee. "Turning on the television to watch Animal Magic and have Freda beaming back at you, the poor kids would have nightmares."

Maud laughed, "Sometimes, sister dear, you can be rather acid with your comments."

Enid tutted, "As if you aren't yourself."

Maud chewed her toffee and decided to leave well alone.

* * *

"How does it feel to be back doing your usual bookings?" Alfred asked Donna as they sat in the hotel lounge enjoying a light lunch of sandwiches and crisps.

"It is a bit strange," said Donna. "Of course, they are all pleased to have me back and it was wonderful of Rita to provide them all with other acts to cover my absence. I did enjoy playing at the Sands. It was really great to be working with other people and not all on my own. It was that which lead me to drinking as much as I used to."

Donna had told Alfred about her problems with alcohol.

"Well perhaps Rita's Angels can find you more theatre work. There is bound to be something else before next year's summer season at The Little Playhouse."

"That's a nice venue too," said Donna. "I know it is small, but I think I would feel a real connection with the audience, like I do when I am playing the clubs."

"I will let you into a secret," said Alfred. "I have never told anyone this, not even my wife, I always wanted to be on the stage, but somehow the hotel got in the way and I had to carry on what my family had started. That is one of the reasons I kept the Little Playhouse going. I'm not in a show, but somehow I feel part of one. I get quite excited when I see people going into the auditorium and reading their programmes, wondering what they are letting themselves in for."

"You are funny," said Donna.

"And you are very beautiful, my love, and more talented than you realise."

"Thank you," said Donna looking at Alfred as he took her hand and kissed her for the first time on the lips.

Sadie Casalino who had popped into the hotel to see Minnie Cooper about something saw the pair in the bar and smiled to herself. "Wedding bells before very long," she thought. "I knew I was on the right track."

* * *

"But why have you chosen Acle," asked Joe, looking at Charles. "I thought you would have found somewhere nearer here."

Charles looked at his friend. "I chose Acle because it was just far enough away. It will give you the space to think about whether or not you want a relationship with me. While I am still in the vicinity, it is difficult for both of us."

"I am so sorry, Charles. I didn't mean to drive you away. I have explained before about the business, this is all I have and I have worked hard for it to be a success."

Charles had long since realised that the two of them moved in very different ways, it was one of the reasons he had given up his vocation to God, in the hope that it would spur on Joe to make a decision. His suggestions about helping Joe at the park and living there with him had drawn a blank and he knew in his heart that Joe was scared of commitment and being judged by others.

"You can come and visit me," said Charles. "You have a car now, one that actually works."

"Yes, thanks to you, Charles."

"I am leaving at the end of the week, I gave my landlady notice. The cottage is ready for me to move into and I have bought myself a motor scooter; I used to ride years ago but gave it up when I moved here as everywhere seemed to be in walking distance."

"Won't you be cut off out there?" asked Joe, who was secretly worried that Charles was doing this for all the wrong reasons.

"No of course not, there are village shops. I will have my scooter and there is the railway station nearby, I can always go into Norwich."

"Or into Great Yarmouth," added Joe

Charles nodded in agreement. "I won't come and see you again before I go so this is by ways of a goodbye."

Joe held out his hand to shake Charles's. He watched as his friend left the park and then turned to look at the place he called home and wished he had had the courage to be with Charles, whom he loved dearly, but had been afraid to tell him.

When Joe called in at Tidy stores Phil had already heard the news.

"I am so sorry Charles has left the area," she said, weighing some cheese for Joe. "I wish you had taken me up on my offer to come over for a meal."

"Sorry about that, I was so busy with work that I completely forgot to mention it to Charles. I do feel bad that he has gone, but I really don't think I could have committed myself to a relationship."

Phil wrapped the cheese in greaseproof paper and sliced some ham. "I hope you are going to keep in touch with him."

"Well, Acle isn't a million miles away and I do have the car now," said Joe, "but at the moment I am concentrating on Finnegan's. It has taken me a long time to improve the site and it needs my continual attention."

"Have you thought of bringing in a site manager, someone to manage affairs when you aren't there?"

"I think it is too early for me to be taking someone else on. I have to start making a good profit first. I have a good cleaning team, but I am the one who looks after the maintenance of the site; it costs a lot to bring someone from outside."

213

Phil totalled the figures. "That will be six pounds please Joe."

Joe handed over the exact money. "I'll be seeing you, thanks Phil."

"Joe, if you ever need someone to talk to, I'm always here. You can still come over for a meal one evening. Don't think you have to muddle through on your own."

Joe smiled. "Thanks again Phil, I'll let you know."

As Joe left the shop he ran into Martha Tidwell. "Acle of all places, whatever possessed him to move to Acle!" She directed this outburst at Joe.

"I really don't know Mrs Tidwell, I am sure he had his reasons."

Martha gave Joe a cold stare "And I have a good idea what they were."

Joe excused himself and hurried back to Finnegan's Wake. He waved to Roberto who was overseeing a delivery of beer from Lacon's, for two pins he would have begged a large whiskey from him, but thought better of it and put the kettle on to make a coffee instead.

Chapter Eleven – November

M r Romsey was writing his staff reports and called Tara into his office. "Please have a seat. Now, tell me honestly, are you enjoying the work?"

Tara, who felt she was beginning to find her feet, nodded sagely. "Oh yes, very much. I do enjoy helping people and the other members of staff have made me feel very welcome."

"I am very pleased to hear that," said Mr Romsey. "I have to say that I have had some very good reports about you and it is not something I would normally do at this stage of the game, but I am going to increase your hourly rate of pay. You won't be earning quite as much as the others as they have been here longer, but I believe you have proven yourself. I will have the rise backdated to your start date so you should receive a nice surprise in your next wage packet."

"Oh, thank you very much," said Tara. "That is very kind of you."

"I believe in rewarding good workers and I am sure that, in time, I will be able to give you your own set of keys to the shop; Daisy and Richard have a set each as I am sure you are aware."

Tara nodded.

"At Christmas time we like to give our staff a bonus and I am pleased to say that you will be entitled to one with the others. We will be closed Christmas Eve, returning to work on the 27th of December and also closed on New Year's Day, but we will be open on New Year's Eve until three in the afternoon."

"That sounds okay," said Tara. "Will it be a paid holiday?"

"Oh yes," said Mr Romsey, "and it doesn't affect your holiday allowance in any way. Now just one thing, I know you travel in from Acle, usually on the bus, will you be able to get in okay or will transport be a problem?"

"I think I should be okay, besides I am sure my boyfriend will be able to drive me in and pick me up afterwards if need be."

"If you need any help with anything, please do not be afraid to ask."

"Thank you, Mr Romsey," said Tara as she got up to leave.

"Thank you, Tara, and keep up the good work."

Jake was very pleased to hear Tara's news. "You see, I know you were unsure when you first took the job, but you have settled in and they are pleased with you, well done my princess."

"Mum and Dad are thrilled for me," said Tara. "I know they worry about me sometimes. It has been hard on them since Janice died."

"Don't forget yourself," said Jake. "You were twins, after all."

"I do miss her," said Tara. "Will you take me over to her grave on Sunday? I would like to put some flowers on there for Mum."

"We can take your mum too if she is up to it," said Jake.

"Well, we could see how she is," said Tara. "She doesn't get out much now since her illness."

Jake squeezed Tara's hand. "Oh, I forgot to tell you, the little cottage near us has been sold. Nice man, goes by the name of Charles George. Apparently, he used to be the vicar over at

Brokencliff. He's got a scooter, so you will probably see him driving about the village from time to time."

"It's nice that the cottage has been sold at last, it stood empty for such a long time. I must remember to tell Mum when I get in."

"And don't forget to mention Sunday to her. The garage is lending me a car until I can buy one proper."

"Oh, that is really nice of them. You see, we have both had some good news today."

Jake grinned. "Yep, things are looking up, my girl. We'll soon be able to name the day."

"Excuse me," said Tara with a laugh. "I haven't seen an engagement ring yet!"

"All in good time," said Jake. "Now, you best get on indoors or your folks will think you are working overtime."

Jake kissed Tara and she hurried along the path from the barn where Jake had been working, bursting with happiness.

* * *

Muriel retrieved the accounts book from her bag and handed it to Lucinda, "I think you will find everything up to date."

"Thank you, Muriel. I am sure I shall. Now don't let your coffee get cold. I will look over the accounts tomorrow and let you have them back."

There was a silence for a few moments and then Lucinda continued. "Tell me, does Freda do much in the way of cooking, I understand she is providing evening meals now."

"Freda is a very basic cook really which is why she has found the cash-and-carry most useful. I have to say it is a big help to many of us."

Lucinda nodded. "I think we are all in agreement on that."

"Freda isn't great at baking. I remember her feeding some of her rock cakes to some sparrows and I swear those birds never took off for days. They waddled around her garden like they were wearing little lead boots."

Lucinda grinned. "We can't all be good at everything."

"Owlerton Hall has been booked for the GAGGA Christmas party on Friday 7th December," said Muriel. "We have got a ten per-cent discount and I have managed to get a small local band to provide the music."

"That all sounds very good," said Lucinda, who was pleased at how well her committee worked together. "I forget to tell you, I have organised some raffle prizes for the party, so it won't need to come out of funds."

"Are you sure?" asked Muriel surprised. "I am sure we would have enough in the kitty to cover them."

"No need my dear," said Lucinda. "Let's just write it off as a donation from the chairman."

There was a silence between them. Muriel watched Lucinda closely and then spoke to her. "Lucinda, is everything okay? Only, I have to say that you haven't been looking yourself lately."

Lucinda gripped her hands together, she had been meaning to speak to Muriel, had wanted to speak to Muriel, but somehow the right time had never shown itself.

"There is something I would like to discuss with you," said Lucinda, "but not here. I wonder if you could call around this afternoon."

Muriel nodded. "Yes, I think that would be okay, I could get to you about three."

"That would be fine," said Lucinda. "Thank you. I will explain it all then."

Palmer's coffee shop was beginning to fill up with tired shoppers, laden with their fruit and veg from the market and wanting some respite from the crowds before making their way home, and the noise was beginning to bother Lucinda.

"I had best make a move," said Lucinda. "I have to pop into the bank."

"I will walk out with you," said Muriel. "Thanks again for the coffee."

"My pleasure, Muriel," replied Lucinda, picking up her handbag.

Muriel waved Lucinda off and headed towards Jarrold's to buy a writing pad and some envelopes.

There was a loud screech of brakes and a thud. Muriel swung around and, with several others, rushed over to the body lying in the path of a car. A police constable patrolling the market was on the scene; the driver of the car was visibly shaken as he got out of the vehicle.

Muriel froze as her eyes fell on the body. Lucinda Haines was lying motionless on the road.

A shopkeeper called out, "I have rung for an ambulance."

The constable acknowledged him gratefully. "I fear we may be too late for an ambulance."

Muriel walked unsteadily towards the constable. "I know this lady, she is a friend of mine, we were having coffee in Palmer's..." Her voice cracked as tears began to roll down her face. "I am meant to be seeing her at three this afternoon, there was something she wanted to tell me."

News of Lucinda soon began to spread. Freda comforted Muriel who was in shock and did her best for her neighbour and friend. On a more practical side, Erica Warren, secretary of GAGGA (The Great Yarmouth and Gorleston Guesthouse Association) thought an urgent meeting of the landladies be called to discuss the future. However, Fenella Wright, former secretary, and Agnes Brown, former treasurer, stepped in, making Erica think again. There was a funeral to arrange and once that had taken place, the landladies needed to have some time before reaching any kind of decision concerning GAGGA. With Lucinda gone, the vacancy for chairman would arise and Erica Warren had long had her eye on the prize; she intended to bide her time.

"That was a dreadful thing to happen," said Rita to Beverley as they were going over some invoices together. "The poor lady must have been killed instantly. We must find out when the funeral is and organise flowers. Lucinda looked after Ted while I was out working. He died in her guest house."

"Yes, I remember it well," said Beverley. "I would think that the GAGGA organisation must be in shock and of course, Lucinda was the chairman. There was a hit-and-run just outside Norwich the other day, according to Ian."

"Life is a precious thing," said Rita with feeling, "but we never realise it until it is too late. That is one of the reasons I have decided to step down, take a back seat as it were."

"You are very wise," said Beverley, putting a red mark through a duplicate invoice. "They are always doing that, sending out two invoices, I bet they think we won't spot it and pay it twice."

"Perhaps we should draft a letter and send it to the managing director."

"Don't worry, it is on my to-do list. I will get Julie to type it up once I have carefully worded it."

"Well I have no fear about handing the reins over to you, Beverley. You're sharper than a box of knives."

Beverley laughed. "My Ian says something along those lines too."

The funeral of Lucinda Haines was a sombre affair and the church was packed. There was a service with hymns that Lucinda liked and then it was straight onto the crematorium where another short service took place committing Lucinda's body to the great unknown and, as the curtains closed in front of the coffin, Muriel began to cry. Freda comforted her friend as they filed out of the building behind the other mourners and were ferried by coaches to Owlerton Hall where Lady Samantha had laid on a funeral tea free of charge.

"Well," said Erica Warren. "We really should think about having an extraordinary meeting and sort out elections for a new chairman."

Ex-secretary Fenella Wright interrupted her. "I really don't think today, of all days, is the time to talking about such things."

"I agree," said Ruby Hamilton who secretly thought that she should be the next chairman, but she knew that Erica was hoping to take that crown.

Gloria Winstanley was eating a sausage roll and chatting to Ethel Winters. "I think the whole GAGGA thing is a little bit dated now Ethel. It was fine when Shirley Llewelyn first started it all those years ago, but we all know our own business best and don't need the likes of some committee to tell us how we should run things."

Ethel nodded. "Well, perhaps we'll be able to put that to the vote when the time comes. I shall send a note in to Erica and Muriel."

"Mind you, I still think we should have a get-together, once a year," said Gloria, wiping her mouth with a napkin. "After all, us landladies are all in it together."

"I give Lucinda her due, she was a smashing leader. She broke down barriers," said Ethel, giving a little sniff. "When Shirley was in charge, I always thought it was us and them, you understand what I am saying Gloria?"

"Indeed I do Ethel. It was thanks to Lucinda that we got special membership of the cash-and-carry. That has been a boon to my economic climate I can tell you. All those presentations by those linen companies got on my wick."

"On several people's wicks, to be perfectly frank," said Ethel, helping herself to another cheese straw.

Petunia Danger went over and chatted to several people she recognised and eventually found herself in the company of Rita Ricer.

"Such a turn-out, I never knew Lucinda knew so many people," she gushed.

Rita nodded. "Yes, it is surprising how many people she did know, but then being in the guest-house business, it isn't any wonder. Some people have travelled from all corners of the country to be here today."

"I was sorry to hear about Malcolm Farrow," said Petunia hoping to hear some gossip.

"That's most kind of you I'm sure," said Rita. "Now, if you'll excuse me, my old lover, there's a couple of people I wish to say hello to."

Dinah and George Sergeant were dressed in black and Dinah's hat sported a veil that Rita though suited her, although due to the sad occasion wouldn't disclose.

"Oh, Mrs Ricer," said Dinah. "It is a very sad day, a very sad day indeed. I said to George, didn't I George, it's a very sad day indeed."

"You did Dinah," said George raising his trilby to greet Rita.

"When I think of the lovely holiday we had at Lucinda's it breaks my heart. I said to you, didn't I George, we had some lovely holidays."

George nodded.

"I feel sure that Lucinda enjoyed having you stay," said Rita, patting Dinah's arm. "She spoke very fondly of you both."

A tear ran down Dinah's cheek. "Did you hear that George, she spoke very fondly of us? That is so lovely."

"Where are you staying?" asked Rita. "I take it you are not going back home this afternoon."

"We are going to try and get a room somewhere. George and I would like to have a few days here to reflect."

Just then Muriel came over. "I am sorry to interrupt but I couldn't help overhearing that you are looking for somewhere to stay. I know the both of you by sight and how often Lucinda mentioned you, I should be happy to invite you to my house."

"That would be most acceptable," said George, surprising everyone.

"Of course, you mustn't worry about payment. I would like to do this for you both and your friendship with Lucinda; she used to say you were her best two guests."

Another tear ran down Dinah's cheek. "Did you hear that George, we were her favourite guests."

Rita smiled at the group. "Well, I am so pleased that you are both sorted. Now, if you'll excuse me, I have to go back to town."

Rita met Jenny outside by the car. "Well, that was something. I wonder if that many people will turn up to my funeral."

"Oh, don't start getting maudlin," said Jenny. "You've years ahead of you yet."

"That's what poor Lucinda must have thought," said Rita, turning the key in the ignition and backing out of the parking space. Jenny silently agreed.

* * *

On the 15th November the Clifftop Players were back at The Little Playhouse in Brokencliff, rehearsing *Wardrobe Doors*. The BBC requested permission to film snapshots of the rehearsals which the company were more than happy to do. The farce was to open on Tuesday 20th November and run until Saturday 8th

December. In discussion with the company it had been agreed that there would no performances on Mondays. The play would run Tuesday to Saturday at 7.30 with matinees on Wednesday and Saturday at 3pm. The BBC had notified the company concerning the two dates they would be filming in full and the first four rows of seats would be removed to allow television cameras to move freely during those times. These performances would be to be an invited audience of locals.

Adding to the excitement, Constance Anderson was interviewed on BBC Look East about the part she played in *Wardrobe Doors* and, in her own unique way, made the interview an amusing one. Also, during the filming period, backstage footage was to be taken along with short interviews with each of the company, to provide a sample of what happens backstage in a theatre before the actual performance.

Advertisements appeared in all the local press, omitting any details of filming. Maud and Barbara were on hand to deal with the bookings and it looked as though putting *Wardrobe Doors* on before Christmas was going to be a success. Several of the company were offered reduced rates to stay at Finnegan's Wake, others had found guest houses in Gorleston, and Constance and William had taken a room at The Beach Croft at a greatly reduced rate. Lady Samantha and Sir Harold invited the company to take afternoon tea at Owlerton Hall; everyone was happy to have some extra business at what would normally be a quiet time of the year.

Jack was very happy to have the company back as they came through the stage doors waving their hellos and asking how he was. He only wished that Milly had returned, but she would be getting ready for her next adventure to Australia with Lauren.

He decided to send her a note and enclose a Christmas card; he would get the address from Rita.

* * *

It was agreed to hold a GAGGA meeting on 30th November to discuss the things that needed airing. The Town Hall had allowed the usual room to be used and as it was such an unusual occasion, they had said that provided everything was cleaned when they had finished, there would be no charge.

As Muriel had been with GAGGA for some years, it was agreed that she would chair this extraordinary meeting, much to Erica's chagrin.

Ruby Hamilton, Petunia Danger, Fenella Wright and Agnes Brown had all taken front row seats. Freda sat with Nettie and Gloria and it seemed that every member of GAGGA had turned out.

"Thank you all for attending," said Muriel. "As you are all aware, we lost our chairman to a terrible accident earlier this month and it is our job here today to vote on how we should proceed. We, that is, Erica and I, have received several suggestions and I would like to read them to you now.

1. That we have an election to vote for a new chairman. Nominees would have to in place by next week. And that until such times as a new chairman is appointed, the meetings to be conducted by me and Erica jointly.
2. That GAGGA is disbanded as it is seen as old hat now.
3. That should GAGGA fold, we agree to hold an annual get together at Christmas to catch up with each other

Further comment - We are capable of running our own businesses and now we have discounts in place at the cash-and-carry, we don't need to waste our time attending meetings. We all know each other and can call on each other if we need help.

"That seems to sum up the feelings of all present and I think at this point it may be a good idea to have a vote on what we have heard."

A murmur went around the room.

"On point one, to have an election for a new chairman, with Erica and I holding the fort until then. A show of hands please."

Only fifteen hands went up.

Muriel looked at Erica who was shocked.

"Can I just say something?" said Gloria "I think maybe we should vote on option two, that GAGGA be folded."

Hands shot up around the room and it appeared that over three quarters of those present were in favour.

"I have to say I am deeply shocked by the show of hands," said Muriel.

"You asked us to vote and we are doing that," shouted out Nettie Windsor. "So get on with it."

Rather shakily Muriel asked for a show of hands on option three and the whole room raised their hands.

"Well, I think that seems to be that," said Muriel.

Erica stood up. "Are you ladies absolutely sure that you wish to see this organisation shut down? It has stood you all in good stead for many years."

"Sorry love, but you only joined us a few months ago," said Gloria. "You come from the Richard's Hotel in Bournemouth as we all know, so why you are so wound up about GAGGA

227

folding or not, I find hard to understand." There followed several 'hear hear's from around the room.

Fenella Wright stood up. "Speaking as someone who served on the committee for many years as secretary I am afraid I have to agree with the majority. I have considered this, long and hard, since the passing of dear Lucinda, and Agnes and I are both of the opinion that this kind of organisation has run its course. When Shirley ran GAGGA it was done as a competition between all the members. Prizes were awarded each year and sadly it was usually the same people who won."

"At last someone is speaking the truth," said Freda, who felt she had kept quiet for too long. "We all knew what was going on, but no one had the nerve to speak up. I do agree that being a member of GAGGA has given us a few privileges with discounts. The best of these was arranged by Lucinda to shop with a discount at Murdell and Pocock. Yes, I am sure we would all like to meet up once a year to have a little celebration and of course we can rely on each other to give support if needed."

There was a thunderous round of applause and Petunia Danger made her voice heard. "Well said, Freda Boggis! If we were going to vote for a new chairman, I would second you."

Freda blushed and sat down.

"Well I think our business is done," said Muriel. "Your wishes will be respected. Erica and I will send out a copy of the annual accounts and I suggest that any revenue left over is put towards our party at Owlerton Hall this Christmas."

Everyone shouted out in agreement.

"There are refreshments in the usual place for those of you who would like to partake."

"As we've paid for it, we might as well have it," said Gloria, motioning Nettie to join her.

Muriel looked at Erica, shrugging her shoulders. "I cannot believe what just happened."

Erica, who had calmed down from her earlier outburst, nodded. "The lion was allowed to roar and it did, loudly."

Muriel left the platform and walked over to Freda. "That was quite a speech you gave Freda, I never realised you felt so passionately about things."

"Well sometimes things need to be said and I decided that today was the day," she said, picking up her bag from below her chair. "Let's grab a cup of tea and a biscuit from here and then I will help you clear up. Afterwards I suggest we treat ourselves to some chips on the market followed by a large schooner of sherry in Divers."

Muriel turned to Erica. "Would you like to join us, Erica?"

Erica shook her head. "I'll go and get the accounts together. You two go on, but thanks for the invitation, it is appreciated."

And so that was the end of GAGGA as it once was.

When Muriel arrived back home she kicked off her shoes, hung up her coat and sat down on the settee. She reflected with some affection on Lucinda and how over the years they had been friends instead of rivals. Her tears began to fall, she sobbed and thought how fragile life could be. She made a promise to herself to treat every day with respect and to help those around her and not see them as a threat. She heard Freda singing next door and decided to do right by her friend less she was lost too.

Chapter Twelve – December

On Friday 7th December, the GAGGA Christmas Party went ahead at Owlerton Hall, paid for by courtesy of the late Lucinda Haines. The evening was well attended and Lady Samantha put in an appearance to say a few words, wishing everyone a merry Christmas. She knew that the organisation was now folding and she secretly thought that, with all that had gone before, it was a wise decision.

Drinks flowed, the buffet table groaned with the variety of food on offer and everyone took to the dance floor and enjoyed themselves.

Fenella Wright and Agnes Brown looked on at the scene before them. "I have to say this really does make a change from the old days," said Fenella smiling.

"You mean when Shirley organised everything to suit those she favoured most. Lucinda did bring a lot of change to GAGGA and I think we all saw that. I am truly sorry Lucinda is no longer with us, she was a good sort."

"Yes, she was," agreed Fenella, "though I think many thought differently until she became our leader. The gloves were well and truly off then and she made sure that we all felt a part of things. There was no hidden agenda."

"It's a shame GAGGA is no more, but then we all took a vote on it and it turned out the way most thought it should."

"The person it hit the hardest is Muriel. Lucinda didn't have what anyone of us would term as close friends but, in Muriel, I think she'd found one."

Agnes nodded. "Yes, you are quite right. I did think that Muriel would have made a good chairman."

"But she would have had competition from Erica Warren. It was quite obvious to me that she had her eye on the prize from the moment she arrived in Great Yarmouth after running such a prestigious hotel in Bournemouth."

"Yes, I always thought that was a bit strange," said Agnes. "She is a strange one and no mistake."

"Come along, let's go and find ourselves somewhere to sit; my feet can't take much more of this standing about."

Ruby Hamilton had abandoned her husband who was dancing with Ethel Winters and, to her mind, making a right sow's ear of it. She sipped her port and lemon and was joined by Petunia Danger.

"Your husband is doing some moves on that floor," said Petunia. "It's amazing how quickly men can move after a few sherbets."

Ruby winced; she hated that kind of reference.

"Are you doing anything special over Christmas?" asked Petunia enjoying what would be her fourth gin and tonic.

"Paul and Petra are coming to spend Christmas with us," said Ruby, pleased she could steer the conversation away from the antics on the dancefloor.

"I didn't know Paul had a dog," said Petunia

"Oh, Petra isn't a dog," said Ruby hurriedly. "Petra is his wife."

"Wife!" exclaimed Petunia. "I didn't know your Paul was married, you kept that very quiet."

"And so did they," replied Ruby. "We only found out two weeks ago."

"I bet that went down well."

"Well, you know what these youngsters are like."

"Your Paul is hardly young, at least 30 to my knowledge; he used to knock about with those boys from the estate."

Again, Ruby winced. "Well, that was a long time ago. He has changed a lot since then."

"Obviously, if he didn't even tell his parents he was getting wed. Where did they meet?"

Ruby smiled. "Paris, they met and fell in love in Paris."

"Very Mills and Boon," said Petunia who thought she just might have another gin. "What does she do for a living?"

"Petra is a dancer by profession."

"Don't tell me, she's a Bluebell girl."

"She dances in the Folies Bergère," said Ruby. "As you can imagine, my side of the family isn't too happy about it and, as well as not being invited to the wedding, it really hasn't gone down too well at all."

"Is she Parisian?"

Ruby felt herself beginning to blush. "Petra's from Huddersfield actually."

"Huddersfield, really, I bet that came as something of a shock."

Ruby drained her port and lemon.

"Give me your glass, Ruby, I'll get you another drink, you look as if you could do with one."

Petunia returned with the refills and handed Ruby a very large port and lemon.

"So, what do Petra's parents do, are they in business?"

"Of sorts," said Ruby, taking a large gulp. "Her father is in refuse and her mother works in a shoe shop."

"That's interesting, what sort of refuse is her father in?"

"Rag and bone to be exact."

Petunia stifled a laugh. Obviously, the drink had loosened Ruby's tongue. She wouldn't normally give so much away. Petunia could hardly wait to get down the wool shop and spread the news.

"Her mother is the manageress of Freeman, Hardy and Willis."

"Well, you'll be okay for a discount on shoes, Ruby and no mistake."

Ruby shuddered, as if she would go to such a shop for her shoes. She prided herself on going to Garlands in Norwich and Palmers in the town, not just any run of the mill operation. "I think I'll just go and powder my nose Petunia. Excuse me please."

"Well, it does look a bit red," said Petunia. "I'll guard the drinks."

Muriel looked on, not drinking, at the party going on around her. She still couldn't get her head around what she had witnessed. The vision of Lucinda lying in the road would haunt her for many a day to come.

Barry, seeing his wife's distress, suggested they leave early and Freda, sensing that her friend and neighbour wasn't up to any kind of celebration, dragged Dick away from the bar and followed suit.

Freda took Muriel's hand and squeezed it. "You need your bed, my friend, it has all been rather too much."

Barry smiled at Freda. "Thanks, Freed you're a good pal."

Saturday 8th December

The final performances of *Wardrobe Doors* took place and the theatre was sold out for both performances. Lady Samantha sent flowers and bottles of wine to the company and congratulated them on their success, adding in her hand-written card that she looked forward to seeing the televised version which was to be shown on Boxing Day. Alfred once again held a small party for them and said he was looking forward to them returning the following year when he felt sure business would flourish. In discussion with the company and Alfred, Ray had said he wanted the company to perform three plays in a week and to that end asked that the Little Playhouse be available in the evening for a performance at 7.30 with the view to giving three matinees, Tuesday and Thursday at 3pm and Saturday at 4.30pm.

This would mean that a Variety Show would not be included in the running.

Monday 10th December

Rita sat in her office looking over some details for a forthcoming show that the agency had been asked to put together and looked up as Beverley came in.

"Rita, there is someone here to see you."

Rita looked at the clock, it was getting late and she and Beverley had been working to get things shipshape for their proposed hand-over the following year.

Beverley hesitated. "It's Malcolm. Malcolm Farrow is here to see you."

Rita dropped the pen she was using. "Malcolm!" she exclaimed.

"I can send him away," said Beverley.

Rita thought for a moment. "Give me a moment and then send him in."

"I'll be right here if you need me," said Beverley.

Rita nodded. She combed her hair, checked her makeup, put her glasses on and made herself look busy as she heard the door open. She looked up slowly and could see the highly polished shoes, the immaculate grey trousers and smart top coat and then the face which had come to her in dreams.

"Thank you for agreeing to see me," said Malcolm, calmly walking towards the desk.

Rita removed her glasses and looked him in the eye. "You've got a nerve, me old lover, walking in here as if butter wouldn't melt. You had better sit down. I have no intention of standing up."

"There is a lot I need to explain," said Malcolm. "It was all lies, all those things she said about me, all lies, don't you understand? Lies, lies, lies…"

"Rita, it's me, Jenny."

Rita opened her eyes. "Where is he, why am I here?"

"You've had a bad dream. The doctor says you are to have complete rest and I am here to ensure that is what you do."

"I don't understand," said Rita, who was feeling fretful and confused.

"You had a terrible shock," said Jenny. "This has been building up for months."

"How long have I been at home?"

"A couple of weeks, but you'll soon be on the mend."

"But the agency, there was a pantomime to sort out, a Christmas show for the Sands…"

"Beverley has taken care everything. Bob Scott has been down to give her a hand; the agency is ticking over nicely. Norman has been running the London office and, according to Bob, has more than proven his worth. Now, let me sit you up and I'll bring you a nice cup of tea."

"What's the time?"

"It's breakfast time. Elsie is downstairs in the kitchen preparing some poached eggs on toast for you."

Jenny helped Rita sit up and placed some extra pillows behind her. "It all seemed so real."

"When you are well enough, Elsie and I are going to take you away on holiday, a cruise perhaps. It will bring the colour back to your cheeks. I'll go and get the tea."

Rita looked around her bedroom, the curtains had been opened and she could see a robin sitting on the tree outside the window, he was chirping away merrily.

"Oh Ted, how did I ever get to this?" she said aloud.

Jenny returned with a cup of tea. "Now, when you have had your breakfast, the doctor thought it would be a good idea to get you up and about."

"Have I been in bed long then?"

"Long enough," said Jenny. "Now drink your tea and Elsie will bring your breakfast shortly. I will lay out some clothes for you and after you have had a warm bath, you'll start to feel better I am sure."

Two hours later, Rita was sitting with her feet up in the lounge and the doctor came to make a call. "You have given everyone quite a worry," he said taking her temperature and pulse. "I rather think that this latest affair on top of you losing your husband and the demands of the agency have taken their toll."

Rita nodded. "I don't think I have ever got over losing Ted. The business kept me busy and taking time to grieve eluded me."

"I am going to leave you a few pills, they are to help you relax, but only take them if you begin to feel anxious, and they can be quite addictive."

Rita thanked him.

"I can arrange some counselling if you think that would help," he smiled. "Sometimes it is good to get things off your chest with a complete stranger."

"That's very kind of you, but I have my friends to talk with. With their help I know I can get through this."

"If you change your mind…" said the doctor. "Now, I will come back and see you in a couple of days. Your friends have said they will take you out for a drive so you can get some fresh air. I have no doubt you will be back to your old self by New Year."

"Thank you very much," said Rita. "Sorry, I don't know your name."

"It's Lucian, Doctor Lucian Farrow. Now, I will leave you to rest. Goodbye Mrs Ricer."

"Everything okay?" asked Jenny as she came into the lounge.

"I think so," said Rita. "He said his name was Doctor Lucian Farrow."

Jenny smiled. "You must have misheard him. His name is Darrow, Dr Lucien Darrow, look it's here on the pills he prescribed."

"Oh, for a moment I thought…"

"Now, how do you feel about going down to the Sands and watching a rehearsal for their Christmas show?"

Rita nodded. "That sounds like a good idea. Will June be there?"

"June has returned to Australia; the theatre is now in the capable hands of Jamie and his staff. June did call in to see you before she left, but you were asleep and she didn't want you disturbed."

"How is Elsie doing at the shop?"

"Oh, great guns," Jenny replied. "The business is doing really well and her Christmas stock doesn't consist of any nativity figures with wonky eyes."

"Oh yes, I remember those," said Rita. "Maud used to say that Elsie got them at knock-down prices, they were rejects."

Beverley arrived in the car to collect Rita, and Jenny and they set off to the Sands.

Feeling the sea air on her face for the first time in weeks, Rita took a deep breath. The covered walkway down the centre of the pier kept the elements at bay, the North Sea was looking particularly angry and waves were crashing against the side of the pier.

Jamie Dormy welcomed the party to the theatre and showed them into the auditorium. Mona Buckle came forward and greeted Rita. "It is very good to see you up and about Mrs Ricer, you have been in my thoughts and prayers."

"Thank you, Mrs Buckle," said Rita.

The party sat down in the fourth row of the stalls and watched the rehearsal which was in full swing. Rita didn't recognise any of the acts and was greatly impressed by the programme that Beverley had obviously had a hand in putting together.

Later back at home Rita had a chat with Beverley about how things were going and then as she began to feel tired, Beverley made her excuses and left Rita to rest.

"She is looking much better," she said to Jenny as she headed for the car.

"Yes, thank goodness, said Jenny. "There have been some moments when I thought we would never get the old Rita back."

* * *

Tuesday 11th December

"Thank you for coming to see me," said David Jarrett. "As you are now aware, I am acting on behalf of the late Lucinda Haines."

Muriel fumbled nervously with her handbag.

"It is my job to deal with Lucinda's last will and testament. She has left you her guest house and the contents within."

Muriel was shocked. "Are you sure there hasn't been a mistake?"

"I can assure you there hasn't been any mistake. When Miss Haines spoke to me she made her instructions very clear. Can I ask you, did Miss Haines speak to you at any time about her health?"

Muriel shook her head. "The last thing she had said to me was there was something she wanted to talk to me about, but privately. I was supposed to meet with her on the afternoon of the accident."

"Then there is a letter I have to give you which I think will explain the situation." He handed her an envelope.

Muriel took the envelope and was about to open it, but decided to put it in her handbag for later.

"Miss Haines had no family and she has left some monies to various people and charitable organisations."

"But what am I going to do with another house?"

"You could always sell the property," suggested Mr Jarrett. "Or you could sell your current home, I understand that Miss Haines's property has been done up to an exceptional standard."

"Yes, it has," agreed Muriel, still feeling very shaky inside.

"There are some other things I would like to go through with you," said Mr Jarrett. "It shouldn't take very long."

Muriel nodded. "I am in no hurry."

Later in the quiet of her own lounge, Muriel opened the letter from Lucinda.

Dear Muriel

If you are reading this then you will know that I have died. I wrote this letter to you in September when I learned from my doctor the news I had been dreading, but was half expecting. I had been feeling unwell for some months but not had it checked. Tests at the hospital revealed that I had advanced cancer and by the time this was discovered they were unable to give me any treatment. You can imagine the shock I felt, but in my usual fashion I managed to keep it to myself.

My GP suggested I should talk to a friend and it had been my intention to talk to you as I regarded you as my closest. I thought I would be able to turn to you. That conversation never took place which is why you are reading this letter and I am sorry.

You will know by now that I have left you my guest house, but you must not feel obliged to keep it if you feel uncomfortable. I was assured that it would fetch a good price with all the improvements. You will reach your own decision on what you would like to do.

I would like to thank you for being a good friend and helping me when I took over GAGGA, I appreciated that more than you may have realised.

My very best wishes

Lucinda

As Muriel began to wipe away her tears, she realised she had a lot of serious thinking to do which, in time, she would discuss with Barry. It was all too much to take in.

Friday 14th December

Maud put down her knitting. "I hear that Rita is on the mend."

"Well, that's good," said Enid, discarding the crossword she was doing. "I have to say that that poor woman has had her fair share of knocks."

"I think Lucinda Haines's funeral probably tipped her over the edge," said Maud, tutting as she dropped a stitch. "Shall I get us some tickets for the Christmas show at the Sands?"

Enid looked over the top of her spectacles. "Oh, I don't think so dear. There is no one on that bill I recognise. I was hoping for someone like Donald Peers or that nice girl off the telly, Dusty something or other."

"I don't think either Donald Peers or Dusty Springfield would want to spend the weeks leading up to Christmas at the end of a pier in the North Sea."

"No, I suppose not," said Enid. "What's the pantomime in Norwich this year?"

"I'll have to check the paper," said Maud. "I'll never get this cardigan finished in time for Christmas."

"Who is it for anyway?"

"I thought it would suit Barbara."

Enid looked at the wool her sister was using. "Do you really think green is her colour?"

"Well, it was on offer at the wool shop."

"I'm not surprised," said Enid with feeling. "I'll go and peel some sprouts."

* * *

Muriel answered the door. "Oh, hello Freda, come in. I'm just finishing the ironing."

"I wondered if you fancied a run over to Lowestoft in the car," said Freda. She had been concerned about Muriel who hadn't been herself since the Lucinda accident.

"I don't think I have anything I need to get from Lowestoft."

"We don't have to go shopping, we can a have a walk along the promenade and maybe have some lunch in Tuttle's, what do you say?"

Muriel folded the teacloth and smiled. "You are a good friend, Freda Boggis."

Freda smiled.

"Let me finish these few bits off and I'll go and change."

"I'll finish those off for you," said Freda. "You go and get changed; that way we can be on our way in no time."

Muriel smiled. "I'll leave you to it then, Freda." She went upstairs to get herself ready.

Muriel and Freda enjoyed their walk along the promenade and although there was a breeze from the North Sea, it was pleasant enough. When they had had enough, they walked back to the town, had a look around some of the shops and, as Freda insisted on paying, they had lunch in Tuttle's.

"She could be a funny bugger," said Muriel, "but she was a good person on the whole."

Freda nodded. "Yes, Lucinda had her faults but, as you say, she was a good person. I wonder what will happen to her guest house; I don't think she had any family to speak of."

"Maybe she has left it to charity," said Muriel, stirring her coffee while trying her best not to reveal what she knew. "Dinah and George Sergeant said they would be lost not being able to go and stay at Lucinda's. I offered them my guest house, but I

244

think they are resigned to never visiting the town again. George was saying that maybe a change would do them both good."

"I've got some news," said Freda, thinking it was time they changed the subject. "My Dick has got a job, a proper job."

Muriel dropped her teaspoon. "Your Dick, a proper job!" she exclaimed, somehow the words didn't seem to go together.

"Murdell and Pocock were looking for a couple of warehouse workers and a friend of his and he decided to apply, and they were both offered a job. Mick, that's Dick's mate, knows the warehouse manager and he has agreed to give them both a three-month trial; they start on Monday."

"Well, that is a surprise," said Muriel, recovering from the shock. "Dick will have to get used to keeping regular working hours."

"And it will keep him out of the Legion," said Freda, with a smile.

"Well, I am pleased for you both," said Muriel, thinking that, not before time, Dick should have gained proper employment.

When they had finished their coffee, the two had a look around the store and then headed back home with Freda driving her red Mini proudly.

"I have to say," said Muriel. "Things have been changing all around this year, haven't they?"

"Oh yes," said Freda. "Even the government have had a hand in things, Value Added Tax, day light robbery if you ask me."

But as Muriel and so many like her knew, the likes of the little people never got a say in anything.

Christmas plans

Rita was beginning to feel much better and had ventured in to town on her own. She was fed up at home and needed a change of scene.

"It won't be quite like the old days, but I thought that I would invite Maud and Enid for Christmas lunch with you and Jenny," said Rita, looking around Elsie's shop. "It would be great if I could get Dave and Dan down here from Blackpool, but they are now making over their home at a guest house in St. Anne's."

"I don't know them that well," said Elsie, "but I have heard that they are a lovely couple of young men."

"Oh yes, they are that alright," said Rita. "I think I will take these, they will make nice gifts for the tree and I'll have a couple of packs of wrapping paper and a couple of rolls of tape please Elsie."

Elsie busied herself and rang the items on the till. "This VAT is causing price rises, but I suppose the government needs to make a few extra pounds."

Rita laughed. "There is always someone wanting our hard-earned cash. Now, let me see, I should have some change here to give you the right money."

Elsie took the cash and handed Rita her purchases wrapped in a nice paper bag, advertising the shop.

"I forgot to tell you, Owlerton Hall is having a Christmas bazaar on Sunday if you fancy coming along. It opens at eleven and runs through until four."

"Oh, that would be a lovely idea," said Elsie. "Then I shall book us a table for lunch at the Beach Croft, my treat. Will you let Jenny know?"

"I will, Elsie and thank you. Now I had best get back to the office, I have some paperwork I need to look at; there are some acts that want to go on our books. If I find any that I think are good, I will get Beverley to go along and see them in the New Year with Jenny."

Elsie opened the shop door for her friend and waved her off.

Freda knocked on Muriel's door. "Christmas Bazaar at Owlerton Hall on Sunday, I will drive us there."

Muriel smiled. "That sounds like a nice idea. I hear they are going to have the Salvation Army band playing carols outside and I have also heard that Donna Quinn is putting in an appearance and giving a couple of Christmas classics in the reception hall."

"We will have a nice day out," said Freda. "Dick doesn't want to come along but if Barry wants to, he is more than welcome."

"He says he has some things to do here," said Muriel. "I expect he will be wrapping presents; he likes to do that when I am not around."

"I don't think my Dick will be wrapping presents," said Freda. "He'll probably be down the Legion wrapping his hand around a pint pot, like as not."

"Well, he is starting work on Monday," Muriel replied, "so it will be his last day of freedom, so to speak."

Freda huffed. "Well, yes, there is that I suppose. Now, what about a nice cup of coffee? I've got a couple of custards here."

Sunday 16 December

The Christmas Bazaar at Owlerton Hall was a great success. Lady Samantha and Sir Harold were on hand to greet people as they arrived. The hall was festooned with a tall fir tree decorated in colourful baubles, lights and sporting a fairy at the top. There were gift stalls, confectionery stalls and toy and book stalls, all kindly donated by local businesses. Mrs Yates and a team of volunteers provided refreshments. The Salvation Army played carols in the car park and shook their collecting tins for donations to help the needy.

Donna Quinn gave a performance accompanied on the piano by Maurice Beeney half way through the proceedings.

Monies raised would be donated to a children's charity with a third of the takings going to Owlerton Hall to continue the improvements.

Lady Samantha had provided ten raffle prizes of varying kinds, bottles of sprits, cuddly toys and the first prize a food hamper donated by Murdell and Pocock containing seasonal favourites.

The raffle tickets sold very well and Lady Samantha asked Rita if she would be so kind to announce the winners. It was Joe Dean who won the hamper and his immediate thought was that he would share it with Charles George who he had hoped to see at the bazaar. Phil Tidy also won a prize and Freda managed to win a large fluffy dog which she said she would donate to the hospital's children's ward and Muriel thought that it would be a lovely thing to do.

Thanks to kinder weather, a display of falconry by Kessingland Wildlife Park was seen in the gardens and proved a popular attraction.

Father Christmas arrived on a sleigh drawn by two reindeer courtesy of Kessingland and handed out small gifts to any children present which had been arranged by the generous donations from Palmer's Department Store in Great Yarmouth.

Also in the garden were four kiddie rides consisting of a merry-go-round, a helter skelter, swing boats and a couple of coin-operated galloping horses.

Following the bazaar, Lady Samantha had invited a few friends and volunteers into the hall's dining room for a sherry and mince pie, homemade of course by Mrs Yates. Penge, who was beginning to get used to the idea of his employers opening the hall to visitors, joined in handing round the trays of sherry. Local press and photographers were on hand and it was hoped that the day would be recorded in the *EDP*, *Great Yarmouth Mercury* and *Lowestoft Journal*.

Alfred congratulated Lady Samantha and said that he thought the idea had been a great success just by looking at all the happy smiling faces. Lady Samantha thanked Donna for her contribution and Alfred thought now would be the time to pop the question. So, in front of quite a large audience, Alfred went down on one knee and asked Donna for her hand in marriage. There were loud cheers as Donna accepted and Rita rushed over to wish the couple all the very best.

Phil, who was standing beside Joe, gave him a nudge. "You see what happiness two people coming together brings. Now, get in that car of yours and drive over to see Charles and while you are at it, you can tell him that I am cooking Christmas lunch for the three of us. If Charles doesn't want to stay at the park, I have a spare room he is welcome to."

Joe smiled at Phil. "You really are the best, thank you. I will go and get the car, come back for the hamper and then go over to Acle."

Charles George opened his front door and was delighted to see Joe standing there.

"Come in, come in," he cried. "It is so lovely to see you, let me make some tea and while the kettle is boiling, I'll show you around the cottage."

"I am so sorry it has taken me all this time to come and visit," Joe replied, feeling happier than he'd imagined to see Charles again. They had kept in touch by fortnightly telephone calls and Joe, who had been very busy with the park, had kept promising Charles he would visit. Charles, on the other hand had ridden over on his motor scooter but had never plucked up the courage to go to the park and, instead, had ridden through Brokencliff, had a coffee and a cake at The Toasted Teacake and gone back home again. Seeing Joe now, he chided himself for his stupidity.

"You have made this look very nice," said Joe, looking around him.

"Come upstairs," said Charles. "I've just had a small bathroom put in and with the two bedrooms it is all quite cosy. I haven't decorated the second bedroom yet. I am keeping that as a project for the winter months when there isn't much I can do. Then, when spring comes, I intend to sort out the front and back gardens. I want to get rid of the old shed at the back and have a new one and perhaps a small greenhouse to grow tomatoes in."

Joe was much impressed and as they sat and had tea together, Joe felt less inhibited than when they had been in Brokencliff together; here they were on neutral territory. "How are you finding the other villagers?"

"Most hospitable I have to say," said Charles, pouring a second cuppa for them both. "Everyone is very friendly and I have to say that I am very happy here."

They chatted about how things were progressing in general and Joe told Charles about Alfred's proposal to Donna and also the news about the Golden Sands theatre."

"I must say I am very sorry to hear about this business with Malcolm Farrow," said Charles. "Poor Rita must be very upset."

"The thing is no one knows what has happened to him and although rumour had it that he put his home up for sale in Oulton Broad, turns out to be totally untrue. It stands empty."

"Have they ever found this Pamela character?"

"No, they haven't, she seems to have disappeared off the face of the earth."

Charles wished there was something he could do to help, but he couldn't think what.

"So, will you come and spend Christmas at Phil's?" asked Joe.

"Indeed I will," said Charles. "I will give young Phil a call to thank her. If you don't mind, I will take up her offer to stay in her spare room."

Joe was secretly relieved and Charles, knowing his friend's anxieties, guessed he was.

"Well I had better make a move," said Joe and Charles went out to the car with him.

Joe turned the key in the ignition but the car wouldn't start. "Oh blast, this would happen. I haven't got my tool box with me. I took it out of the boot to put the hamper inside."

"Don't worry," said Charles, grabbing his coat from the hallway. "My friend Jake lives just down the road and even though it is the Sabbath, I am sure he will be more than willing to help you."

Charles returned a few minutes later with Jake and introductions were made. Jake looked under the bonnet and quickly spotted the problem. "Give me a couple of minutes and I'll have you back on the road in no time."

True to his word, the car was fixed, Joe waved goodbye and headed back to Brokencliff.

"Now, you must let me know what you are owed" said Charles. "Joe, in his haste to get home, has forgotten his manners."

Jake shook his head. "Have this on me," he said smiling. "It was nothing really."

But Charles wouldn't hear of it. "No, you must give me an amount I insist."

Jake, who had taken to Charles George since his arrival in Acle, had an idea. "If it's all the same to you, money need not change hands. But you can do me and Tara a big favour and marry us next spring."

"But what about your local vicar? Surely you would want him to perform the ceremony."

"Well to be honest, we don't see eye to eye with each other and I know that Tara would appreciate you officiating the service."

"Yes, she is a nice girl. I would probably have to obtain permission from the powers-that-be to marry you, but I don't think it will be a problem."

"There is just one thing," said Jake. "I haven't asked Tara to marry me yet, I am planning to do it on Christmas Eve when I plan to engage her."

"Well, my boy, you are full of surprises. I shall not say anything to her. I am going to see her mother again soon; I know how much comfort my visits give her."

"Oh, they do. She never stops talking about you, says you are the best thing to have arrived in Acle for many a year."

Tuesday 18 December

Charles George pulled on his overcoat and headed out to the railway station; he was making his weekly trip to Norwich to visit patients who had no relatives at the Norfolk and Norwich Hospital. He would read to them, chat about things of interest and his obvious care about others gave his recipients much comfort.

On this particular day, Matron asked to see him. "It is very good of you to come along here each week. I am sorry to tell you that Mrs York died a few days ago. Mr Jewson has undergone major surgery and he is in recovery."

Charles nodded his head, such news never came as a shock, it was just the way life was, God moved in mysterious ways.

"I was wondering if you would take a look at a patient we have had here for some time. Until last week he was in a coma, brought in following some kind of hit and run. He had no identification on him and we have not been able to get much sense out of him. The police have circulated his details, such as they are, to other stations but are reluctant to release details to the papers which, in my opinion, really ought to be done. He was found by the roadside just outside the city after being hit by a car. I wondered if you could see what you made of the gentleman."

"Of course, Matron, of course. Anything I can to do to help."

Charles looked at the gentleman lying in his bed; his head was partially covered with bandages, but he smiled at Charles and blinked his eyes.

"Hello my good fellow, my name is Charles George and Matron thought you might like a visitor."

The gentleman muffled a thank you.

"Are you able to tell me your name?"

The man shook his head gently.

"Arh well, perhaps it will come to you in time. I live over at Acle, I recently moved there after I gave up my ministry at Brokencliff-on-Sea. A beautiful part of the Norfolk coast, not too far from either Great Yarmouth or Lowestoft.

There was a flicker of recognition on the man's face.

"Perhaps you know Brokencliff?"

Charles could see that the man was struggling to say something and was becoming quite agitated.

"Calm down there's a good fellow. Relax a little, perhaps you will remember another time. I am usually here once a week. I won't be able to visit until next Friday week, as there will be Christmas and I will be staying with some friends in Brokencliff over the holiday period. If there is anything you would like me to bring you, please feel to ask and I will see what I can do."

Again, the man became agitated and reached out his hand to Charles, which Charles took. "Perhaps I can read to you," he said, looking with some concern at him. The man blinked his eyes and smiled again.

"Now I happen to have a book with me, it's the story of a family coming through the Second World War. Let's see if you like it and, if so, I can continue with it during each of my visits."

An hour later Charles went to find Matron and reported what he had seen. "When I mentioned the Norfolk coast there was some kind of recognition in his eyes. It's a shame the police won't put out a description in the press, it might well bring someone forward."

Matron acknowledged Charles "My thoughts too, perhaps I will try again and see what happens, but you know how busy the hospital is and there doesn't always seem enough time to do everything."

"Without wishing to tread on your toes, would you like me to try my luck?"

"That would be most helpful," said Matron "look here is the details of the sergeant I spoke to at the city police station, you can mention my name, Matron Crackenthorpe. You might strike lucky."

Charles stood up to take his leave. "Allow me to wish you a Merry Christmas and I will see you on Friday the 28th."

"I will be here," said Matron smiling "I have pulled the short straw this year, though I will be off for New Year."

"I am sure your patients appreciate you being here during the Christmas holidays."

"I have always hoped so," replied Matron, walking to the door with Charles. "It is a sad time to be in hospital and even worse if there is no one to visit you."

George said goodbye and headed off to the city police station to see if he could work a little magic.

The sergeant welcomed Charles and ushered him into a small room. "Would you like something to drink?"

"Oh, no thank you, Sergeant. I had a drink at the hospital."

"I understand you have come concerning the hit-and-run gentleman."

"Well yes, I met with him today and he seemed to be regaining some of his memory. What I don't understand is, why a description of the man wasn't published in the press, there must be someone out there who would know who this man is."

The sergeant coughed. "We think we have an idea who he might be, but we can't be absolutely sure at this moment in time."

"Can you give me a clue?"

"I have to be very careful what I say here," said the sergeant, "but, as a member of the cloth, I think I have your word that you will not repeat anything I tell you."

"I am an ex-member of the cloth, as you put it, but you have my word I won't tell a soul."

"We believe the man to be part of a team of confidence tricksters. We know that this man didn't work alone. The police have had their eye on him for some time. Basically, he courts women, gains their confidence and then with the help of his accomplice, robs them blind."

"So, do you think that the person who ran him down had found him out?"

"Oh no, we think the person who ran him down was his partner-in-crime."

"There was no identification on him when he was found?"

"That is correct. He changes his identity every now and then, so he may have been in the process of doing that again."

"Do you know where he was last seen?" asked Charles, trying to get a clearer picture in his mind.

"It was in the Norfolk area. The last name he used known to us was Kenneth Strong."

"Strong, that rings a bell Sergeant. Have you heard of a Pamela Strong? I believe I may be able to point you in the right direction. If my hunch is right, the man lying in the Norfolk and Norwich is Malcolm Farrow. There was something about his appearance that puzzled me, I thought I recognised him by his eyes. I remember a lot of people like that."

"I best get a desk sergeant in here to make some notes. You may be on to something, I want you tell me all you know about Malcolm Farrow."

* * *

Wednesday 19 December

"I really am at a loss of what to buy my Dick," said Freda as she found a space in Palmer's car park. "Though I suppose some new shirts wouldn't go amiss; men can be so difficult to buy for. I might see if there is a new aftershave out, I expect my friend will be on the market today, he usually does most days leading up to Christmas."

"Have you never thought of buying him some Old Spice or Brut?" asked Muriel getting out of the car. "Those things you buy off the market aren't very pleasant."

"Aren't they?" queried Freda, locking the car door and dropping the keys into her bag. "I quite liked the last one and he seemed to."

"Well some people are easily pleased," said Muriel. "Now where to first? I want to go into Jarrold's and get a book for Barry, but I can go there after we've been to Palmer's. Barry has started to enjoy reading adventure stories. I thought I might chance buying him a James Bond story."

"I thought he was only a fictitious character," said Freda. "I didn't realise he wrote books."

"Oh Freda, James Bond is a character created by the author Ian Fleming."

"I thought he discovered penicillin," said Freda, offering Muriel a humbug.

Muriel looked at her friend aghast. "Oh, Freda what are you like?"

"I don't think Dick would enjoy a James Bond, he is more into cowboys and Indians and war things. Perhaps Jarrold's will have a Roy Rogers annual."

"You're going back, aren't you?" said Muriel, stepping out of the way of a muddy puddle.

"Well, I can't know everything," said Freda shaking her foot after not missing the puddle. "Oh, look at that, all over my new boots."

"It will clean off, just watch where you are walking, that rain in the night has left its mark."

"Yes, all over my new boots," said Freda, not best pleased.

"Can I get you anything in Jarrold's, a book perhaps, for Christmas?"

"Come to think of it I've not long finished reading *Nicholas Nickleby*, oh that was a sad tale and no mistake, those poor boys at Doodlebug Hall were treated very badly and that boy Smike, such a shame he died when he did."

Muriel laughed to herself. Trust Freda to get it all wrong, Doodlebug Hall indeed. "Would you like another Dickens to read then?"

"I've read *A Christmas Carol* and *David Copperfield*."

"You might like *Bleak House*," suggested Muriel. "I'll see what I can come up with. It will be a nice surprise Christmas morning."

The two went on their way happily into the warmth of Palmer's where they looked around, had a coffee and then carried on with the business of Christmas shopping.

Christmas Eve

"Thanks for picking me up Joe, I was intending to catch a train later, but this is so much more convenient."

"That's absolutely fine," said Joe, putting the small suitcase into the boot. Charles also had a carrier bag of wrapped gifts which he kept with him in case some fell out on the journey. "Phil is all ready for you and is looking forward to your visit."

"I wonder if you might detour and stop by Rita's Angels, I would like to have a quick word with Rita Ricer and I would sooner do it in person."

Joe drove down the Acle straight with some Christmas music playing on his car radio. They arrived in Great Yarmouth and Joe parked near the market place. "I am going to go and find a couple of things in the newsagents. I'll meet you back here at the car in say, half an hour."

"That will be ample time," said Charles, walking across the road. He entered the hallway of the building and made his way to the first floor.

"Reverend George, this is a surprise," said Rita, greeting him warmly, "or do you prefer me to drop the title."

"Call me Charles," he said, sitting down. "You must wonder why I have come to see you."

"It did cross my mind. Would you like some tea or coffee?"

"No, I am fine, thank you. I am on my way to Brokencliff to spend Christmas with Phil Tidy and Joe Dean. The reason for this visit is that I have some news that I would rather you heard from me first, I think you had best prepare yourself for a shock."

Rita looked worried. "Oh, my goodness. What are you about to tell me?"

"It concerns Malcolm, Malcolm Farrow. I know where he is and I know what he is."

Rita felt the colour drain from her face. "Go on."

Charles explained all he knew and Rita sat as calmly as she could and listened.

"You see, you may well be hearing from the police shortly and I wanted you to be prepared. I felt you had to know as it has affected you greatly."

"Thank you," whispered Rita. "It is very hard to take in. I have to tell you that Malcolm never once tried to extract, or suggest he wanted, anything from me other than my hand in marriage."

"I think maybe he had found his true love," said Charles, "and that may have upset the apple cart with Pamela."

"You say he in the Norfolk and Norwich, so do you think I should try and visit him to get his side of the story?"

"I would advise against it for now," said Charles, "until the police have spoken with you. The fact that the man doesn't appear to remember who he is may be a ploy on his part, or be a fact. I can tell you that when I mentioned this part of the country, recognition of sorts was visible."

"It all sounds so incredible. The man I knew doesn't fit what the police believe of him to be true."

"The sign of a professional confidence trickster perhaps?" said Charles.

"Perhaps," agreed Rita.

"This really wasn't the best day to impart this kind of news, so please forgive me, I only hope that it will not spoil any Christmas plans you have."

Rita smiled. "You don't have to worry on that score, me old lover, my friends will more than compensate for anything I have heard here today."

"I have your word that you will not repeat what I have told you to a living soul. I shouldn't have betrayed the confidence but on this occasion, I thought it only fair that you, of all people, should know."

"You have my word, in fact in some ways it is a bit of relief to have heard this, it will put a few demons to rest in time."

"Thank you for seeing me, Rita and may I take this opportunity to wish you a Merry Christmas."

"Thank you, Charles," said Rita shaking his hand. "And may I wish you and Joe many happy years together."

Charles blushed. "How did you know?"

"My dear man, love always shines a light."

And with that ringing in his ears, Charles left the office smiling and made his way back to meet Joe at the car.

Christmas Day

Muriel rang Freda's doorbell. "Happy Christmas Freda, have you got a minute?"

"Come in Muriel," said Freda, her hands covered in flour. "I've been making mince pies. I've got fed up with those ones from the shop. Dick is in the kitchen, peeling some potatoes."

Muriel followed Freda into the front lounge. "I have something to give you."

Freda took the envelope from Muriel and opened it. "What is all of this, have you robbed a bank?"

Muriel laughed. "You better count it, it is a thousand pounds."

"I don't understand," said Freda, who felt herself beginning to shake. "I have a present under the tree from you, this is way too much."

"I have something else to ask you, how would you feel about moving from here and taking over Lucinda's house?"

"What, whatever does this mean?" Freda felt perspiration running down her face.

"Lucinda left me her house in her will. I don't have the heart to move into it as I spent quite a lot of time there with her. What I am suggesting is that you put your house on the market and whatever price you get, you give it me. In exchange, you take on Lucinda's house."

Freda was stunned.

"I know it is a lot to take on, but if you think you would like to accept my offer, you can let me know. If you do agree to sell this house, we would have to refurbish it to entice any prospective buyer."

"But why don't you just sell Lucinda's house?"

"Because I thought that, as a friend, I would offer it to you first, I know you have struggled running a guest house, but Lucinda's would be a new start for you and Dick. It has been made over to an exceptional standard and has lots of added features that this house doesn't."

"But we wouldn't be neighbours any more," said Freda.

"But," Muriel said, "we would always be friends and help each other out."

Freda looked at the money again, looked at Muriel and didn't know what to say.

In Acle, Tara, with the help of Jake, had prepared an excellent Christmas lunch and it was a joy to have her mother Mary down from her bedroom to join everyone. Her father Matty was on drinks duty and ensured that everyone was kept topped up. Jake's parents had joined the party along with Albert Smith who helped out on the farm. Everyone enjoyed unwrapping presents and then Jake delivered his big surprise and presented Tara with a beautiful emerald engagement ring. They both decided there and then to announce they intended to marry the following spring. Albert used the occasion to announce that he would be leaving the farm and retiring to his sister's home in Devon. She had recently lost her husband and he had decided that the two of them would be company for each other. This would mean that the cottage he lived in on the farm would become free and Tara and Jake could have it as their first home. Mary was delighted for her daughter and looked forward to helping her plan the wedding. It seemed that this good news had lifted her own spirits and she felt so much better than she had done in many a long day.

At Brokencliff, Phil, Charles and Joe ate their breakfast and after washing up, with the turkey in the oven the three went to the living room to open the presents that had been placed under the tree. There were some jokey gifts that made them all laugh and then Charles opened a beautiful wrapped gift from Phil, it was a sliver photo frame with a picture of Charles and Joe standing on the clifftop that she had taken one summer's day. Charles was delighted and Joe grinned, handing Charles a small gift from him.

It was a beautiful St. Christopher with the words 'to my best friend, love Joe' engraved on the back.

Charles had had a similar idea but in the shape of a silver chain bracelet with an inscription of 'May God keep You Safe' on the reserve.

They all went along to the local church to hear the service by the new vicar. Martha Tidwell was also in the congregation and came over to wish Charles a Merry Christmas. Alfred Barton and Donna Quinn were also among the congregation and everyone said what a wonderful service it had been. Reverend Stephen Newman was pleased to see Charles there and the two exchanged words and Stephen was invited to Phil's for a sherry which he accepted with good grace. He was to lunch with Martha Tidwell and Phil was pleased to hear that Martha had at last made progress with her new employer.

Alfred and Donna were joined by several of the staff of the hotel for Christmas lunch and a party atmosphere got underway. Everyone had lent a hand in the food preparation and with no guests in residence everyone was able to let their hair down. Following the three-course lunch, Alfred played Father Christmas, giving out presents to each of his staff. There were whoops of happiness and surprise, he really had pushed the boat out and matched a gift to each.

At the bar he gave Donna a small box and revealed a cluster diamond ring which he placed on her finger. Donna was delighted and then motioning Minnie Cooper to the piano sang a couple of songs for the occasion.

Over at Rita's, the fun got underway when the ladies all assembled in the living room to exchange presents. Enid had a couple of sherries and Maud guessed she would revert to her entertaining self once the dinner was on the table and Enid didn't disappoint.

"You see, the thing about Christmas," she slurred, "is it's Christmas."

Rita laughed and Jenny nearly choked on her starter of melon balls.

"Every Christmas that Mary," continued Enid, "rides on a donkey with her husband Jo... Jose... Joseph walking beside her to find somewhere she can give birth. Is there a hospital nearby or a mid-wife to be found? There is not. That poor woman ended up in an unheated barn surrounded by cattle, shepherds and men on camels."

"So, we are given to believe," said Elsie, taking a sip of her wine. "It is a lovely story."

"I wouldn't want to spend the night in a barn with a load of strangers," said Enid, hiccupping.

"I don't suppose you'll ever be asked," said Maud, smiling. She secretly loved her sister getting a bit merry.

"I'll have you know," continued Enid, "I was approached once in a bus shelter."

"Who was it? Charlton Heston?" Maud laughed.

"As a matter of fact, it was Ernie Smith off the cockle and whelk stall asking if I had a light."

"The plot thickens," joined in Jenny, starting to clear the plates. "Come on Rita, I'll give you a hand to dish up."

"You see," said Enid, "people don't dish up enough these days it's all fish and chips in newspapers. I bet they didn't have that when Jesus was born."

"I don't think the chippy would have opened on Christmas Day in Bethlehem," said Maud.

"I bet them Kings had a packed lunch," said Enid, taking another swig of her sherry and draining the glass. "Pickled eggs and a bag of crisps."

"Best not give her any wine," said Elsie looking at Enid.

"Oh, I'll have some of that," said Enid "Is it Marquis Rosemary?"

"It's Riesling," said Maud, "a fine German wine."

"You see they came good in the end," said Enid. "The Germans, I knew a German once, he let me share his sausage, though he gave it another name, can't quite remember what it was called now."

"It is probably best forgotten, me old lover," said Rita, carrying in the turkey ready for carving. Jenny followed in with tureens of vegetables.

"Bratwurst," added Elsie.

"No, it was quite nice," said Enid, with a puzzled look on her face.

"My word, that looks a feast," said Maud.

"Jenny, will you carve?" asked Rita. "I am not too hot on that kind of thing."

Jenny began to carve the white meat. "Anyone want a leg?"

"I've got two of my own, thank you very much," added Enid who was really getting the taste of the wine. "Mind you, the doctor says I need to keep them up when resting, get my circulation going or something like that."

Rita went to get the cranberry sauce and gravy. "Everyone please help yourselves to vegetables. Maud, you best serve Enid's for her."

"I want stuffing," said Enid, and everyone burst out laughing as Enid slid gracefully to the floor.

Friday 28 December

Charles walked onto the ward and was greeted by Matron Crackenthorpe. "Please come into my office," she said.

Charles sensed that all was not well and sat down.

"The police came to see our mystery man," she said, fidgeting in her chair, "and I believe some progress was being made. When they left, I checked in on the patient to make sure he was okay. He seemed to be much as usual. However later that evening he was showing signs of distress. A doctor examined him and called upon another for a second opinion; it appeared that he had pneumonia. The doctors did all they could but, I am sorry to tell you, the gentleman passed away during the early hours of this morning."

"Oh dear," said Charles. "Did anyone else come in to see him?"

"Oh no, he had no other visitors other than you and the police. I understand they were getting prepared to release a statement to the press."

"I believe I know who he was."

"Really, who was he?"

Charles told his story and Matron nodded in the appropriate places. "My goodness, quite a story, we had no idea."

"The police were going over to visit Mrs Ricer, but said they would leave it until the New Year."

"Will you tell her what has happened?"

"I think it best that I do. I will have another word with the sergeant after I leave here."

Matron smiled. "That would probably be best."

"Now, who have you got for me today?"

"There is a Mr Arthur Sidles who came in a couple of days ago. He is a spritely old gentleman but he has had a couple of falls and dislocated his hip. He will be with us for a couple of weeks until we can get him into a home. You see he has no surviving family. I understand he is very religious and also likes gardening and anything to do with aircraft."

"Then I would be the perfect visitor. Is there anyone else you would like me to visit?"

"Miss Hinks, she is quite lonely and is here after undergoing cancer surgery. She is very chatty but, like Arthur, has no family to speak of. She likes to listen to *The Archers* and *Woman's Hour*."

"Well I'm a great *Archers* fan, so we'll have something in common."

Matron led the way, grateful that people like Charles were willing to give up their time to do a hospital visit.

Charles enjoyed visiting patients at the hospital and had extended this to visiting people in Acle who he had discovered were not able to get out very much and had no family to speak of. He felt that he was continuing to do God's work without the constraints of a dog collar. His calm and mild manner was something people warmed to and his neighbours had embraced. People often waved to him as he went about his business on his motor scooter. Charles felt very comfortable with his new life and he was so grateful that he had been able to follow a new path.

Saturday 29 December

When Charles caught up with Rita at her offices, she had already spoken with the police. "Quite a tale they had to tell," she said to Charles, "and in some ways a relief. I had thought of going to visit him but in hindsight I am pleased that I didn't. It would have only upset me and perhaps this way is the best way."

"Would you like me to find out the funeral arrangements?"

"Thank you but no. I have been to enough funerals and one more would not be welcome. I have so much to keep me busy and I would sooner be doing that."

"I will probably go along," said Charles. "Would you like me to take any flowers for you?"

"Again, thank you Charles, but no. What has happened has happened and it is best I leave this well alone now."

"I totally understand," replied Charles, getting to his feet. "I am going to catch the train over to Brokencliff. Joe and I have some sorting out we need to discuss."

"That sounds good," said Rita. "Look, I can give you a lift if you like, I have to go over and see Alfred Barton, he wants to put a programme in place for The Little Playhouse and now seems as good a time as any."

"Most kind Rita, thank you."

"So, what are you and Joe planning if you don't mind me asking?"

"He has agreed to come and live with me and put in a caretaker at the park for next year. Chances are Joe will go over there every day to see that all is well; it's his baby after all."

"Well that is good news," said Rita following Charles out of the office.

"It's all down to Phil. I think she must have talked some sense to him. We had such a lovely Christmas together and I'd like to think we could make a stab at living together."

"I am sure you will both do very well," said Rita, taking her car keys from her bag and opening the door for Charles.

* * *

"So, Roberto," said Sadie. "I have had a word with Alfred Barton and have agreed that we put on a New Year's Eve party here. He said that he will pay for the food which can be prepared and ferried over from the hotel. We can lay on the drinks and Donna, bless her, has agreed to do a few numbers. That housekeeper Minnie Cooper will be playing the piano by all accounts."

"I will sort out some bunting from the cash and carry," said Roberto, looking forward to the evening, "and I have some news for you my love, the boys are coming home to visit. They arrive tomorrow."

Sadie gasped in surprise. "My bambinos, Andrea, Durante and Gerardo all here with me and Papa to celebrate the New Year. I will have to prepare some rooms."

Roberto hugged his wife "I will give you a hand my darling, come along let's be having you."

* * *

Ann, Bea and Cissy Brown looked at the invitation to join the New Year's Eve Party that had come through the door at The Lawns.

"Perhaps we should go to be neighbourly," said Bea, admiring the gilt lettering on the card.

"We don't go in for that sort of thing," said Cissy, being her usual cranky self.

"Well, maybe it's time we did, we might have some fun."

Cissy looked at Ann. "What do you think?"

Ann thought for a moment. "Well it wouldn't do any harm. There will be food, so we won't have to cook anything for ourselves here. There will be drink and entertainment and, let's face it, we listen to the wireless every New Year's Eve and it is

271

the same old thing. I don't mind Scottish country dancing, but it gets a bit boring."

Bea clapped her hands together. "Well, for once, sisters we are going out to enjoy ourselves and that means you as well, Cissy."

Cissy shrugged her shoulders. "Oh, alright, just this once."

"Now, get your coats and hats, we are going to Lowestoft to buy a new outfit apiece, it is high time we wore something new," said Bea, feeling quite elated by the thought.

The other two looked at each other and followed their sister to the door. They actually felt quite excited at the prospect but didn't like to show it.

* * *

Later on, Rita had laid out some food as Jenny and Elsie arrived. They were planning on having a quiet evening together. Rita told them about the invitation she had received to The Fisherman's. "And I thought we could all treat ourselves and stay overnight at The Beach Croft, I have sorted it with Alfred."

"That's a lovely idea," said Elsie. "I am closing the shop until the fourth of January. Need to do a little stock-take. Perhaps you could give me a hand, Jenny?"

"A pleasure," said Jenny, helping herself to a sandwich. "Now I have some news for the both of you and you will not believe it."

"Go on," said Rita and Elsie on the edge of their seats.

"Audrey Audley is back," said Jenny

"As what dear, a clown?" said Rita remembering her last reincarnation as an interior decorator calling herself Sandie Cross.

"She has gone into business with her friend Rueben Roberts. They are opening an Acting Academy in Norwich and she has managed to regain her old office in the city. Now you are going to love this, she is calling it Audrey Audley's Acting Academy and Artistic Agency."

Rita burst into fits of laughter. "My goodness, has that woman got no shame? Don't tell me she will be playing all the parts of her staff herself. It is hilarious, that has to be the funniest thing I have heard in a long time."

"Can you imagine it? AAAAAAA! How on earth will someone be able to answer the phone with that mouthful?" said Elsie, who could see the funny side of it. "Good morning, this is Audrey Audley's Acting Academy and Artistic Agency, I'm Anna, how can I help you?"

Rita had tears running down her face. "Oh, please stop, my sides are hurting."

"You have to admit she has more front than Blackpool," said Jenny, giggling. "The girls got wind of it at a meeting and couldn't wait to come back and tell me. I've been holding onto that bit of news for days. The look on your faces is a picture."

Sunday 30 December

Mona Buckle made her way along the pier to the Golden Sands Theatre and entered with her pass key. She could hear some of the backstage boys who had come in to do spot checks. Today was Mona's late-arrival day; at least two days a week she gave herself the opportunity of a relaxing morning, but never the same days each week. The arrangement was working well. Very often she would encounter the agency cleaning staff and catch them out on unscheduled breaks. Mona took her job very seriously and would not stand for any nonsense.

She took off her hat, filled her bucket with water and waddled to the backstage area to see what needed doing. Edwin and the backstage boys always waved to her and, in their own way, had become very fond of her. It wasn't long before the echoes of *The Old Rugged Cross* could be heard and everyone was certain Mrs Buckle was in a happy mood. It would be tea and bourbons at eleven as usual.

Jamie Dormy was particularly happy with Mona and had got used to her strange little ways. She was polite and a hard-working individual. His secretary Cheryl said that Mona reminded her of her late grandmother, although she was Chinese, had the same attitude as Mona and she too had her favourite song that she hummed or sang day and night.

New Year's Eve

It seemed that Brokencliff-on-Sea was the place to be on New Year's Eve. Roberto and Sadie Casalino had kept the pub closed during the day so that they could be ready to open their doors at eight that evening when their guests would begin to arrive. They had been joined by their triplet sons Andrea, Durante and Gerardo who were giving their parents a hand with the preparations. Sadie was in her element. Not only was she looking forward to the evening, but having her sons there too made everything extra-special.

Joe had collected Charles from Acle at Phil's insistence; they had had such a good time over the Christmas holiday she thought they should celebrate New Year together and join the throng at The Fisherman's.

Stephen Price had put skeleton staff in place, with a few supplied by an agency, so that his staff could also enjoy the festivities. Rita, Jenny and Elsie were going to stay overnight at The Beach Croft. Donna had been rehearsing that morning in the basement of the hotel and was accompanied by Minnie Cooper on the piano. Donna had found a couple of new numbers and wanted to try them out before she sang that evening.

Alfred was upstairs in his apartment, laying out his clothes for that evening. He picked up the photo frame containing his ex-wife Jean and looked at it. "Well, we have both come a long way in a short time," he said and just then his private line rang. It was Jean calling to wish him a Happy New Year. He decided to tell Jean his news about Donna and she was delighted for him. "You must come over for the wedding if you can," he said. "I'll let you know when it is."

Jean said she would see, but in her heart of hearts knew that she wouldn't, for Alfred's sake, attend the wedding. It needed to be a new start for him and she didn't have any claim on that. She would send a gift and a card at the appropriate time.

They chatted for a few minutes and said their goodbyes. Alfred took the photo frame and put it in the bottom drawer of the dresser, some things were meant to be.

Donna had been doing some thinking about her forthcoming marriage and told Alfred that she didn't really want to live at the hotel, or 'living over the shop' as she put it. Alfred said that he totally understood and they would keep their eyes peeled for a house in Brokencliff should one become available. It had been decided that it would be a Church wedding and Donna would wear white. Alfred said she was to find a dressmaker who would design the kind of gown Donna would like to wear and she decided that she would approach Rita as she might know of such a person. Maud was very pleased for the pair and thought Donna and Alfred made the ideal couple, a sentiment agreed by many that knew them. Lady Samantha had come forward and told Alfred that she would be happy to hold the wedding reception at Owlerton Hall and, as Alfred wanted as many of his staff at the ceremony as possible, agreed it would be an ideal venue providing his future wife was in agreement, which she was.

Minnie Cooper had decided to have a new hair style and had booked an appointment at Mr Adrian's in Great Yarmouth. Adrian was wearing black from head to toe and a black bandana. He explained to Minnie that he was in mourning for Lucinda Haines who he looked upon as a friend and confidant. "She was like a mother to me," he said. "An absolute doll of a woman. I simply adored her."

Minnie nodded she had little knowledge of Lucinda so she went along with his sentiment.

"Now, I will get one of my girls to give you a wash and condition. I can see you have a lovely head of hair, plenty to play with. I would like to suggest a few streaks of burnished beechnut and some light blonde streaks to bring out the effect. We can keep the hair just above the shoulder and give it a high lift on the top.

276

Kelly Marie who had only joined the salon a month before had managed to almost drown Minnie; there was water everywhere.

Mr Adrian minced across the floor, full of apologies. "Kelly Marie who are we expecting this afternoon, Esther Williams?" Minnie managed to laugh at this.

"I don't know," said Kelly Marie doing her best to towel dry the mess she had made. "Shall I check the bookings book?"

"No dear, that won't be necessary. Now I will sort out this muddle, you can take yourself off and make Miss Cooper a nice cup of coffee."

Kelly Marie looked down at the floor and wandered off.

"I am so sorry about that Miss Cooper. Let's get you over to my station and get started."

* * *

Maud and Enid were planning a quiet evening at home with a light supper, a couple of drinks and the television. Maud had got a bottle of sherry in and also a small bottle of gin and some tonic water. Enid had made some sausage rolls and cheese straws earlier that day and Maud had prepared a couple of sandwiches.

"I was thinking," said Maud. "We ought to have another little holiday in the New Year, about March time."

"You are being very free with your holidays," said Enid who was still getting over their trip to Bristol.

"Perhaps we could go somewhere warm."

"If you are thinking of going abroad you can count me out, it's full of foreigners."

It was the answer Maud expected to hear and thought she would broach the subject again in a couple of months' time or maybe after Enid had had a couple of glasses of sherry.

Mona Buckle had finished her work at the Sands for the day and was heading home when she ran into Beverley as she reached the exit to the pier.

"Oh, I am so glad I caught you Mrs Buckle," she said with a smile. "Ian and I are going over to The Fisherman's in Brokencliff tonight and I wondered if you would like to come along with us. Mrs Ricer and co will be there and it could be a fun evening."

"That is very kind of you, but how would I get there and get back again?"

"No need to worry about that. We have hired a local minibus, so we can all go and return together."

"I expect it will be a late evening," said Mona, thinking. "I don't know if I would stay awake and my leg has been giving me gyp today, it's all to do with the cold."

Beverley smiled. "Well if you have a little rest when you get home I am sure you will be fine. We could pick you up about eight. Now I have the car with me, so hop in and I'll give you a lift home. Here, let me take your bags for you."

Mona was quite overwhelmed by the kindness being shown her as Beverley opened the passenger car door to allow her to get in.

"I quite miss coming into the office," said Mona, as Beverley pulled away from the kerb. "But the Sands keeps me busy, oh yes it does."

"It will be lovely to have you with us this evening," said Beverley. "Mrs Ricer, Mrs Stevens and Miss Benjamin will be thrilled to see you."

Tears began to fill Mona's eyes as she thought of what she had planned for that evening, a meal of shepherd's pie and vegetables left over from the day before, a bottle of stout and then a bit of television before going to bed. Now she would be in the company of others and feel that she belonged.

Beverley dropped her off and took her bags to the front door. "See you at eight, Mrs Buckle."

Mona opened her front door and the silence was as deafening as usual. She turned on the wireless and one bar of the electric fire and went to fill the kettle. She lit the gas oven and put her dinner in to warm through. She decided that she would eat first, have a little nap and then take a bath. While the kettle was boiling she went upstairs to her wardrobe to see what might be suitable to wear. During the summer she had treated herself to some clothes in the sales and pulled out a blue frock with a high neck, some low-healed, black court shoes and in her dresser drawer she found her ruby stone broach and a string of pearls with earrings to match. New Year, she thought to herself, new outfit. She had also purchased a new winter coat which was black and in keeping with her usual attire.

She went back downstairs and retrieved the mail from the doormat. She poured hot water on the tealeaves in the pot and laid the corner of the kitchen table with a cloth. The radio cheered her and when she had finished her refreshing brew she took her dinner out of the oven, removed the covering plate and set it on the table. This would be her first new year without

Bertie and although they had rarely celebrated together, but they did have each other's company at least.

She washed up her dinner things and then went upstairs to have a short rest. An hour later at the sound of the alarm clock she went to the bathroom to run her bath. She had been given some bath salts and Morny Soap for Christmas and she decided that this was the time to make use of them. The bath was warm and she wallowed in the scented water. The soap gave a good lather, much better than the household soap she usually managed with. She washed her hair with some shampoo that had also been a present and pat dried it with a towel. She intended to finger wave it and as it had been recently cut, she found this easy to manage.

She came down the stairs wearing her new outfit, she had removed the bandage from her leg and had put on a pair of tights, something she didn't normally bother with, but with the shoes and the new dress she wanted to look her best. She went to her dresser in the kitchen and took out a bottle of sherry and poured a large measure into a glass. There was half an hour before her lift would arrive so she enjoyed sipping her drink as she hummed along to the tunes on the radio. She caught a glimpse of herself in the mirror and returning to the dresser drawer she got out a bag of makeup that had barely been used. She put a teacloth round the front of her shoulders and decided to apply a little rouge, some powder, a smearing of blue eyeshadow and some red lipstick. Unaccustomed as she was to such things, she managed to do a reasonable job. She looked at her hands, her nails were clean and besides she didn't have any nail varnish so they would have to do. As she put the makeup bag away her attention was drawn to the voice on the wireless.

"And now a special request on New Year's Eve for Mrs Buckle of Great Yarmouth, here with best wishes from everyone at the Golden Sands, Lena Martell sings The Old Rugged Cross."

She sat down with her sherry and stared at the wireless, tears pricked her eyelids and for the first time in many years, she felt very special indeed.

* * *

Freda and Muriel were going to accompany their husbands to an evening at The Star Hotel which was putting on a bit of a do. Some of the other landladies were also going to be there but, as Muriel reflected, it wouldn't seem the same without Lucinda. There promised to be a buffet, a live dance band and a guest singer.

Freda had been busy at her sewing machine and had made a long dress, in deep purple that was adored with sequinned ducks and geese. She had found the velvet material on offer in Palmer's and the sequined adornments, purchased on the market, had to be hand-stitched on the finished article. She had dug out a fox-fur stole she had purchased at a Church jumble sale and although it had the smell of mothballs, it wasn't moulting. The fox's head had two crossed, beady eyes and the brush was a mixture of red and brown. She had got Dick to spray paint her evening sandals in lilac and they had been drying in the shed for the past week. She had her hair in large curlers and her face had the remains of a face pack she hadn't washed off properly which Dick was happy to point out to her.

She emptied her silver evening bag and sifted through the contents, discarding used tissues, a rather worn-down lipstick and several hair grips. Muriel had offered to do her makeup so she wouldn't be attempting that and was grateful of the offer.

Dick had collected his one-and-only suit from the drycleaners and Freda had made him buy some black shoes, socks and some underwear. Barry was lending him a bowtie.

Muriel arrived at 6:30 with her case of makeup. Freda was wearing her dressing gown and Muriel set about applying a foundation to Freda's face. She blended in some dark purple eyeshadow, light rouge on her cheeks and her lips in a black tulip hue. A dusting of face powder completed the look. Freda was very pleased with the outcome and went upstairs to change into her outfit.

Muriel was wearing her hair in a bun and her shimmering gold gown and matching bag and shoes set her off a treat. Dick commented on how lovely she looked. Barry had given her a necklace and earrings for Christmas which she was wearing much to his delight. She had manicured her nails and had applied a light-pink nail varnish.

Freda came thundering down the stairs in a state of excitement and entered the lounge beaming from ear to ear. "Well, what do you think?"

Muriel looked at the dress in disbelief. "Freda you appear to have sequinned ducks and geese on your frock."

"I know," said Freda. "They are super, they really set it off I think."

"I am sure that Old MacDonald's wife would have loved it," said Muriel and then, wishing she had kept quiet, blushed, but

Freda was in her element and hadn't taken in what Muriel had said.

Freda slipped on her newly sprayed shoes which still seemed to be a bit tacky and would no doubt stick to her tights until she undressed later. Then she put on the fox stole, feeling very proud of her outfit.

"Freda, did you know that fox is cross-eyed? Aren't you afraid it will attack the ducks and geese?"

"My mother used to say that if you met a cross-eyed man it would bring you good luck."

"I wonder what she would have said about foxes," said Muriel.

"Oh drat, I haven't put on any perfume," said Freda. "I'll have to go back upstairs now."

Muriel rifled in her evening bag. "Oh, please don't, I have some Estée Lauder in here, it smells divine, here spray some on your neck."

"I was going to use my new one, Wild Coyote Aroma. The man on the market says it's been his best seller this year."

"I'm sure he does," said Muriel offering her bottle of Estée Launder to Freda who, she was pleased to see, sprayed her neck with it.

"Oh, that does smell nice," said Freda. "I shall feel like a proper lady now."

"Even if you do look a proper Charlie in that get-up," thought Muriel to herself. She would always be the same old Freda and even though she had decided not to take on Lucinda's house, Muriel wouldn't have changed her friend for the world and that was how she felt friends should be.

* * *

THE END

The Epilogue

- 1974 would see two weddings; Jake to his beloved Tara in the early spring and Alfred to the lady of his dreams, Donna in June. Charles George was granted permission to officiate both ceremonies.

- Rita finally took a back seat at Rita's Angels and Beverley took full charge of the agency, putting her own stamp on things.

- Owlerton Hall continued to prosper as did The Beach Croft Hotel.

- Joe Dean saw his bookings escalate at Finnegan's Wake and with a resident caretaker in place he was able to live in Acle with Charles for five nights of the week, the situation suited them both well.

- Muriel sold Lucinda's guest house and she put some of her inheritance aside for a rainy day and used some to treat Freda, Dick, Barry and herself to a holiday in London staying at The Kensington Gardens Hotel with a couple of theatre visits included. Muriel was interviewed by the local press about the folding of GAGGA; she felt it was the least she could do in the memory of Lucinda who, she stated, without her guidance the association couldn't have continued. This certainly got up the noses of one or two of the landladies.

- Elsie Stevens made a great success of her gift emporium with the help of Jenny Benjamin.

- The Golden Sands Theatre was in use all year around with visiting shows and musicals and saw the return of the Twice Nightly summer season that had once been its forte with Donna Quinn sharing the top of the bill. Following the successful season, Donna was offered her own television show on BBC Two. As the critics said, "Donna connects with the real people and sings the songs they want to hear."

- Lauren Du Barrie toured Australia for 35 weeks in *Hello Dolly* with Milly doing at least two of the performances each week. The publicity machine had gone into overdrive with Lauren and Milly being interviewed on television and in the press.

- When they returned to the UK, Lauren decided to retire feeling that she had gone out on a high and promised to complete her memoirs, as suggested by Milly, to be called *It's the Voice You Know*.

- Milly left Lauren's employ and decided to go out and taste Saturday's high life as the song suggested in Dolly. She eventually found herself back in Norfolk where she met Jack the stage doorkeeper again and the two decided to settle down together. Milly never went back on the stage.

- The Clifftop Players returned to The Little Playhouse and appeared in *Wanted*, *One Body*, *The Fire in the Attic*, and *Murder in the Back Passage*. The season proved to be a sell-out.

- As for Audrey Audley, well I couldn't possibly say... but there was talk...

I was asked for the words of the hymn that Mona Buckle always sings, so here it is... (and for the record it was my late mother's favourite)

Words & Music: George Bennard, 1913 (MIDI, score).
The Old Rugged Cross was written in Albion, Michigan. Or Pokagon, Michigan. Or Sturgeon Bay, Wisconsin. All three towns claim to be the birthplace of this hymn.

On a hill far away stood an old rugged cross,
The emblem of suffering and shame;
And I love that old cross where the dearest and best
For a world of lost sinners was slain.
Refrain
So I'll cherish the old rugged cross,
Till my trophies at last I lay down;
I will cling to the old rugged cross,
And exchange it some day for a crown.
O that old rugged cross, so despised by the world,
Has a wondrous attraction for me;
For the dear Lamb of God left His glory above
To bear it to dark Calvary.
Refrain
In that old rugged cross, stained with blood so divine,
A wondrous beauty I see,
For 'twas on that old cross Jesus suffered and died,
To pardon and sanctify me.
Refrain
To the old rugged cross I will ever be true;
Its shame and reproach gladly bear;

Then He'll call me some day to my home far away,
Where His glory forever I'll share.
Refrain

(This works better if you have a galvanised bucket and mop
beside you)